For Jim

ICE TRACKS

TODAY'S HEROIC AGE OF POLAR ADVENTURE

by

ANGIE BUTLER

ERSKINE PRESS
2008

ICE TRACKS

First published in 2008 by
The Erskine Press, The White House, Eccles, Norwich NR16 2PB

WWW.ERSKINE-PRESS.COM

Designed by Lodge Graphics Ltd.

ISBN 978 1 85297 100 7

Front cover: Erling Kagge
Back cover: Rune Gjeldnes

CONTENTS

Ilushin-76 Novo Base

ACKNOWLEDGEMENTS

I was researching the Edwardian explorer, Frank Wild, at the Scott Polar Research Institute when I struck up a conversation with the eminent Polar historian, academic and author, Dr Beau Riffenburgh. Hundreds of books have been published on the Edwardian 'heroic age' but no-one has written a book on present day Polar adventurers. I have Beau to thank for this book. It was with his wonderful encouragement and my complete naivety of the task that lay ahead that I took up the challenge. I have met ordinary people who have achieved the extraordinary as well as many present day Polar greats and it has been a privilege. I am profoundly indebted to them for giving me so much of their time and sharing their stories and photographs, their triumphant highs and their moving lows.

To Dr Victor Boyarsky, Ann Daniels, Conrad and Hilary Dickinson, Sir Ranulph Fiennes, Rune Gjeldnes, Erling Kagge, Mike Horn, Paul Landry, Matty McNair, Borge Ousland, Geoff Somers MBE, Rosie Stancer, Dr Mike Stoud OBE, John Wilton-Davies, Sarah McNair-Landry, Eric McNair-Landry, Dr Mikhail Malakhov, Robert Swan OBE and Richard Weber: their daring and dash upholds the true spirit of adventure and flies the flag for human endeavour

Special thanks must go to the Norwegian posse of Erling Kagge, Rune Gjeldnes and Borge Ousland for giving me unlimited access to their superb photographs, many of which were taken during hair-raising moments.

Having commenced the project I found myself faced with a mountain that needed to be scaled yet I had no prior knowledge of mountaineering. My heartfelt thanks go to Paul Landry, my friend and adviser, who continually handed me ropes, picks and crampons each time I teetered on the edge. Unbounded thanks goes to my publisher Cris de Boos who has shown immeasurable patience as I zigzaged my way uphill and was there to greet me at the top.

My thanks goes to Jill and Mike Cable who continued to encourage me and shared their vast knowledge of the vagaries of the publishing world. I also thank Robin Benger in Toronto for his optimism for the book and Bar Kinghorn in Spain who continually assured me with the words, 'I never doubt for one moment that you will achieve what you set out to do!'

I must give recognition to all my friends at the Scott Polar Research Institute, in particular Heather Lane, Naomi Boneham and Lucy Martin who have supported me with their loyalty.

Tom and Tina Sjogren, no mean adventurers themselves, having conquered the 'three' Poles,(North, South and Everest), have provided me with a wealth of information from their encyclopaedic web site, ExplorersWeb.

I am indebted to Robin Ollington and Frank Lee of Lodge Graphics for capturing the very essence of Polar adventure through their design of the book. I am most grateful to Pippa Upfill-Brown for her skilled editing job.

I thank all my wonderful family and friends, too many to name, but they know who they are, who have spurred me on with cheers of encouragement; and my oldest friend, Tiki Kyte, who continues to provides me with footholds.

Finally, incalculable thanks go to my girls, Kate, Rosie, Saskia, Candida and Aurelia, who surround me with love and constant riotous entertainment.

I dedicate this book to Jim, my rock, who for the past thirty years and more has supported all my projects, ventures and wanderings and has an unshakeable belief in everything I do.

THE ARCTIC (where penguins don't live)

The North Pole (geographic) is situated in the middle of the Arctic Ocean, which in turn is flanked by parts of Canada, Greenland, Russia, USA (Alaska), Finland, Sweden, Norway and Iceland. This area is known as the Arctic Circle.

In winter the Arctic Ocean normally reaches approximately 9.3 million square kilometres before shrinking to about 4.4 million in the summer. However recent evidence shows that the ice cap shrunk to just 2.6 million square kilometres, the smallest it has been in recorded history. It is predicted that the Arctic could become ice free in summer in 20 years time.

Walking to the North Pole, particularly from the Canadian coastline, is considered more difficult than the South Pole for several reasons. Obstacles include 'negative drift' (currents that sweep the ocean ice, and anyone on it, away from the Pole). The Arctic Ocean's constant movement causes the surface ice to separate and close, creating streams of water called 'leads'; at the same time pressure ridges, jumbled blocks of ice reaching 15 metres high, form as the ice converges on itself. In addition there is the threat of Polar bears.

It is believed that at least a fifth of the world's undiscovered oil and natural gas reserves lies beneath the Arctic Ocean.

No country owns the Arctic Ocean or the North Pole; however, countries surrounding the Arctic have limited exploitation rights within an exclusive zone. Each country has ten years to make claims to extend their zones.

The battle of ownership hots up between the United States, Russia, Canada and Norway. Russia has been accused of 'unlawfully' annexing the Arctic for control of oil and sea-lanes by sending in nuclear powered icebreakers to patrol the much-coveted icy waters.

THE ANTARCTIC (where Polar bears don't live)

The Antarctic is often described as the coldest, windiest, and driest continent in the world. Surrounded by the Southern Ocean it covers 14 million square km and is covered in an ice sheet 1.6 km thick. It is roughly circular, except for the Peninsula, an 'arm' that protrudes from the North West. It is the Peninsula that covers 4% of the continent which is most affected by global warming and as a result has lost 'calved' large ice shelves such as the Larsen B ice shelf. The rest of Antarctica, 96%, has had a stable temperature over the last 40 years. During the winter the size of Antarctica doubles as the sea ice freezes.

It has no permanent inhabitants, although some 4,000 scientists work on research stations such as the American Amundsen-Scott Base at the South Pole which are spread around the continent

Antarctica is protected by the Antarctic Treaty, presently signed by 46 countries. In 1991 the Madrid Protocol was signed to protect the continent from mining. This moratorium will be reviewed in 2041.

Antarctica, gloriously beautiful, bounded by enormous icebergs and spectacular mountains is growing in popularity as a tourist destination. Nearly 30,000 visitors travelled along the Peninsula in 2007. Most of the tour operators belong to IAATO (International Association of Antarctic Tour Operators) which has strict guidelines to ensure the protection of the coastline and its fauna, that of penguins, fur seals and its flora, mainly lichens, algae, fungi and bryophytes.

The majority of adventurers heading for the South Pole fly in from Punta Arenas in Chile to a base named Patriot Hills although it is possible to fly from Cape Town to the Russian science station, Novo.

The USA has constructed a 1,448 km 'ice highway' from its southern McMurdo Base to the American Amundsen-Scott base at the South Pole.

Besides the cold and the ferocious winds, adventurers are faced with the hazard of falling into crevasses, deep and often hidden fissures that form on glaciers. Still, in spite of their terrifying reputation, there has only been one recorded crevasse fatality in recent history, that of a science research station worker.

POLAR RULES

Since the late 1980s Polar adventure 'rules' and 'records' have swirled about in deep and muddy waters. Before that it was simply a matter to be 'the first and 'to get there and back in one piece'. *How* you did it was immaterial. Today, as the popularity for Polar adventure increases, claims and counter claims of records are fired across the ice fields with increasing velocity. Until Polar adventure becomes an Olympic sport the rules will remain in a miasma of discord. Questions arise. What constitutes going 'solo', 'unsupported' or 'unassisted' etc. on an expedition? Is the use of kites to harness the wind or an evacuation of a team member considered 'assisted'? Does the receiving of supplies during an expedition cancel out the status of 'solo'?

The excellent website ExplorersWeb, the only portal crammed with Polar expeditions and much more, is run by Tom and Tina Sjogren, Polar record-breakers themselves. Besides providing statistics it lays down hard and fast rules as to what constitutes fair play. The Sjogrens, with their acerbic views, are accused of being self-arbiters of Polar policy. Not so, says Tom, who insists the rules have been set down by a collective agreement.

I too have conducted my own collective research with Polar enthusiasts and, needless to say, it mostly conflicts with ExplorersWeb. I hope I have given a reasonable voice to the adventurers in my book. It would be fair to say that the type of character undertaking these challenges is not predisposed to follow rules and, precluding cheating, Polar adventure is all the better for that. As of one of the greatest modern day adventurers, Borge Ousland, says: 'I do the trips the way I want to.'

I have purposely avoided the word 'explorer,' leaving that title for those who set out to map unchartered lands.

GETTING THERE

ANTARCTICA FROM SOUTH AMERICA

ALE (Antarctic Logistics and Expeditions) is the only company in operation that will oversee every detail of your expedition to the South Pole and surrounding areas. The company provides logistic support to almost all expeditions in Antarctica.

In the 2007/2008 season, a three-month window during November, December and January, ALE flew 325 people in 18 flights with an Ilyushin 76 aircraft, from Punta Arenas in Chile to their base camp, Patriot Hills which utilises a natural blue ice runway and was established in 1987. It is the furthest south tented camp in Antarctica and lies 1076 km from the Pole.

From there, adventurers attempting a complete expedition are delivered by Twin Otter to Hercules Inlet on the coast. Mountaineers are taken to Mt Vinson, the highest peak in Antarctica, and scientists are ferried to their various field camps. It is a complicated and demanding logistical exercise.

Patriot Hills is made up of 80 tents and has 46 staff providing everything from accommodation, medical care and fresh food frequently flown in from Punta Arenas.

Its subsidiary, Adventure Network International, runs full guided programs which include flights to look at the Emperor penguin colonies on the South Coast of the Weddell Sea, safaris in the Ellsworth Mountains and guided climbs of Mount Vinson.

www.antarctic-logistics.com
www.adventure-network.com

ANTARCTICA FROM SOUTH AFRICA

ALCI (Antarctic Logistics Centre International) is a Russian run outfit based in Cape Town, South Africa, since 2001. Its flights from Cape Town to the Russian base Novolazarevskaya on Dronning Maud Land takes six hours in an Ilyushin 76TD aircraft. The company also flies Basler Turbo 67 aircraft and a MI-8 helicopter and mainly services the scientific bases in the area. However, it does take on private expeditions as it did with transporting Rune Gjeldnes to the start of his solo Antarctic traverse.

ALCI transports clients from Cape Town to 'Novo' for a company called White Desert, run by the adventurer, Patrick Woodhead. White Desert provides specialized top end camping and skiing trips.

www.alci.info
www.white-desert.com

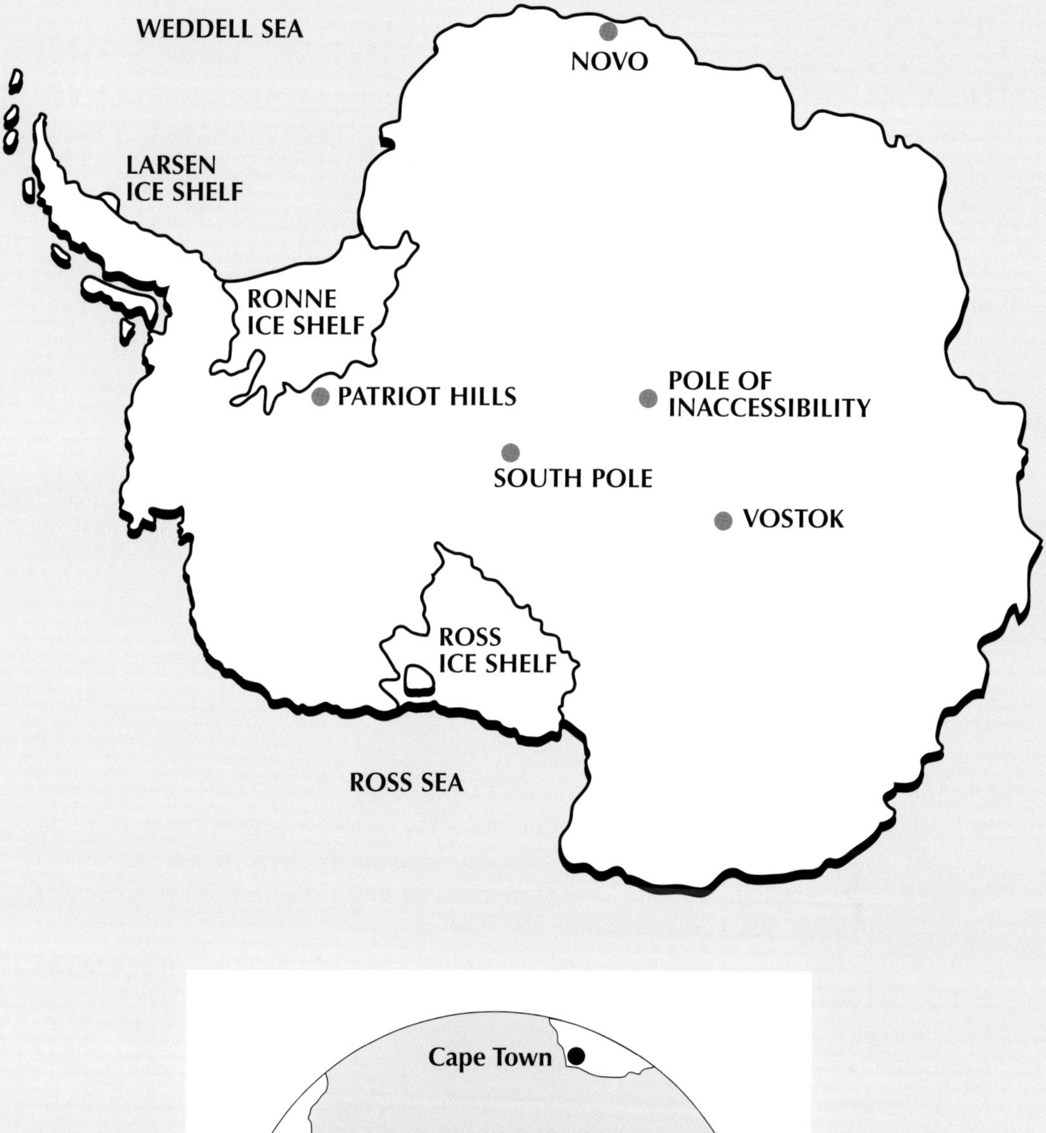

WEDDELL SEA

LARSEN
ICE SHELF

RONNE
ICE SHELF

PATRIOT HILLS

NOVO

POLE OF
INACCESSIBILITY

SOUTH POLE

VOSTOK

ROSS
ICE SHELF

ROSS SEA

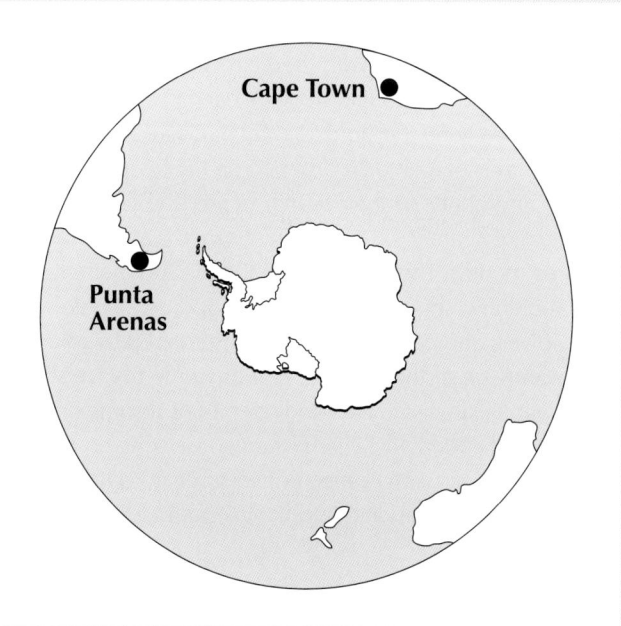

Cape Town

Punta
Arenas

THE NORTH POLE

The two most popular routes to the North Pole start either from Canada, from Ward Hunt Island via Resolute Bay or from the Russian side, Cape Arctichesky, via Svalbard, Norway.

FROM CANADA.

At present the only company operating from Canada is Kenn Borek Air. Its competitor, First Air, famous for its outstanding Twin Otter pilots to whom many adventurers owe their survival, was bought by a young Inuit called Jimmy Onalik in 2002. His operation failed, leaving Kenn Borek Air as the sole operator and in a position to name their price.

Logistically, all the starting points to either the North or South Pole are complicated and everything depends on weather and exceptional piloting.

It takes some five hours to fly from Resolute to Ward Hunt Island Island, the launching pad for the North Pole, stopping on the way for a refuel at a Canadian weather station called Eureka. For flights further north on the Arctic Ocean, fuel drops must be orchestrated from Eureka and a series of bunny hopping of fuel drops and refuelling is necessary. www.borekair.com

---

FROM RUSSIA

VICAAR Ltd, in conjunction with the company Center Polus, is run by one of the doyennes of Polar exploration, the Russian, Dr Victor Boyarsky. The company, besides taking tourists to the North Pole by air and by ship, supplies logistic support in the Arctic for adventurers and scientists and is wholly responsible for the temporary floating Arctic base called 'Borneo' or sometimes 'Barneo' that is created from scratch each year.

The organisational skills required are mind-boggling. In late March some 120 tons of fuel is deposited on Sredniy Island in Siberia to service aircraft ranging from IL-76s to helicopters. Two helicopters depart from Sredniy and with the help of information from scientists of the Arctic Institute in St Petersburg head onto the Arctic Ocean in search of an ice flow to support the first temporary floating base at 86.5∞ North. Simultaneously a cargo plane takes to the air from Moscow carrying five tons of fuel to be dropped on the temporary base in order for the two helicopters to refuel and continue their search nearer the Pole, in the region of 88,5° North, for the perfect piece of floating ice to sustain "Borneo", a base camp that will support a micro "village" for three months. The ice must support a 1200 metre runway, aircraft, tents and during the three month window, possibly two hundred people. As soon as this is established, tractors, skydivers and 20 tons of fuel are airdropped to commence the building of the runway and the setting up of the 'village'. If at any time the ice starts to break up the camp is dismantled, the people are evacuated and operations resume on more stable ice. No one pulls this off better than the Russians who have been working on drifting stations for the past 100 years. In 2008 the floe carrying Borneo drifted some five km in a twelve-hour period and finally crossed the Greenwich meridian into the Western Hemisphere. www.norpolex.com

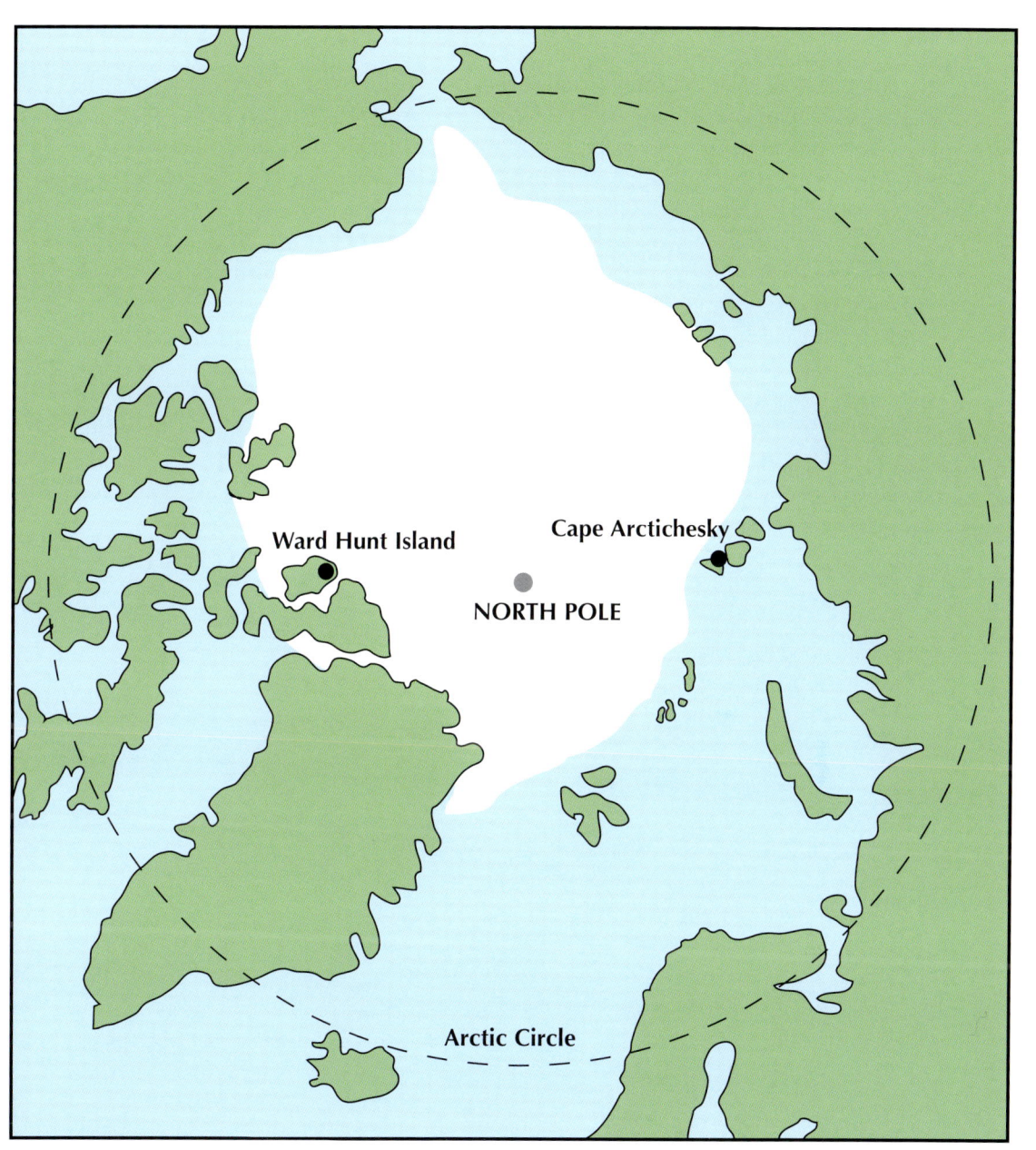

Ward Hunt Island

Cape Artichesky

NORTH POLE

Arctic Circle

THE QUESTION IS *WHY?*

The first question Polar adventurers are asked is "Why?" Often it is the most difficult question to answer and seldom is there just one answer. Polar journeys push one to the limit. They are a risky business, albeit the risks are calculated. To dig deep from a reserve beyond one's reckoning is an addictive drug. Then there is the need to be 'the first', to have one's name gild the record books for perpetuity.

The scale of the Polar regions is vast; no photograph, film or the imagination can portray the splendour of the icebergs, mountains and glaciers in the South or the millions of square miles of shifting frozen ocean to the North.

I sensed a similarity, something interchangeable, between the characters of those choosing a life in a cloistered religious order and those choosing to cross the Poles, particularly those who elect to go solo and unsupported. Many of the people I interviewed agreed. It is as if extreme adventurers and holy men are made of the same material: the need to peel back the layers through isolation, introspection and hardship. Stripping oneself of all comforts and sensory stimulation and communing with Nature brings you closer to spiritual illumination. The methods might be different. The monk chooses a life of passive, quiet contemplation; the adventurer puts himself through punishing physical exertion, but the final state of enlightenment is attained.

Frank Wild, the Edwardian explorer, said,
'Once you have been to the white unknown you can never escape the call of the little voices.'

THE GREAT ROBERT PEARY DEBATE

Robert Edwin Peary 1856 - 1920

One of the most heated arguments amongst Polar historians and adventurers today is the question of who was the first person to reach the North Pole. In 1909 the American, Robert Edwin Peary, assisted by his servant, the African American Matthew Henson and four Inuit men, Ootah, Egigingwah, Seegloo and Ooqueah, claimed the prize. "My dream and ambition for 23 years....mine at last..."

Peary and Henson had long adopted Inuit culture and customs. In fact they both fathered Inuit children. Honoured by his country and Europe for his achievements for Arctic exploration, which were considerable, Peary's claim to have reached the North Pole from Ellesmere Island, is considered by his detractors to be nothing short of heresy, particularly by those who believe the Briton, Wally Herbert, is the rightful conqueror of the Pole. Although he is mostly discredited some steadfastly believe that Frederick Cook's 1908 claim is genuine

Peary left Ellesmere Island on 1st March 1909. A final reading of his position was taken one month later at "Camp Bartlett", before the big push for the Pole. The position was 87° 45'. Bartlett, with the support party, then turned back, leaving Peary, Henson and the four Inuits to conquer the last 155 statute miles. Up until that point the party averaged marches of 21 km a day. Peary claimed to have doubled his speed and reached the Pole in six days. He then quadrupled his speed back to Camp Bartlett. "Impossible" cry the detractors!

Although Peary had dogs and sledges and the most experienced men of the Arctic to assist him, it is not deemed feasible to cover the distance in the time he said it took him and the lack of data to substantiate his claim has simply added fuel to the debate.

In the year 2000, Paul Landry repeated the journey by dog sledge in 42 days, underpinning his belief that Peary's record is justified. Matty McNair and the team she guided, led by Tom Avery, set out in 2005 to replicate Peary's journey. Overall they matched Peary's 37-day claim, but the team did not manage to replicate anything like Peary's final five-day speed average, and that, according to the sceptics, is where the argument falls down.

Whether Peary reached the Pole or in all honesty thought he had or even if he exaggerated his claims, one thing is certain - the argument will never be settled. Peary died in 1920, Henson in 1955 with very little of the recognition he deserved. His remains were finally interred among America's heroes in Arlington National Cemetery, near to Peary's grave, the man whom he had assisted for 22 years.

ROSIE STANCER

"Every journey starts with one step and most people talk about their dreams but they never get any closer than that."

Rosie Stancer is a little pixie. An engaging, ditsy, bright blue eyed sprite who doesn't sit still for long but darts about in bursts of fairy dust. As much as you try and look for a dragon lurking behind the scatty persona, you soon realize she is what you see, which is very polite, self-deprecating, a little vulnerable and a person who appears somewhat surprised that she now finds herself in the position of attempting to be the first woman in the world to walk to the North Pole solo.

The great British Polar guide and adventurer, Geoff Somers, who has trained her in the past, describes her as a scatter-brain, born with a silver spoon in her mouth, who couldn't read a map, light a stove or read a compass and, more indignantly, complains that she will not put on weight. "I use to send her pictures of Sumo wrestlers and say, 'this is how I want you to look when you set off!' She might be a little giddy but one glance at Stancer's record and her remarkable courage stands out.

I met her at the large country house she shares with her husband William, the grandson of James Wordie who was the geologist on Shackleton's Transantarctic Expedition, and their small son Jock. The house is tucked away at the end of a non-descript lane surrounded by farmland and over-looking the beautiful Tollesbury salt marshes on the Essex coast of England.

We sat at the pine table in her cluttered kitchen, surrounded by Jock's paintings pinned on the walls, drinking bog-standard English tea out of the finest china teacups.

We talked around a cacophony of telephone calls, a workman interrupting, the arrival of two men to look over a car she was selling and just when she sat down for the fourth time she jumped up, apologising once again. Would I mind following her in my car to a local sports centre where Jock was at a children's party and we could carry on the interview there?

Due to the preparations for the North Pole offensive and her daily punishing, military based training programme, involving hauling tyres and attacking assault courses, she had barely seen her son. Stancer, mother, wife and Polar adventurer was trying to be all things to all people.

Obviously extremely popular with the local parents, she greeted everyone at the club with a hug. The interview continued in a canteen, our voices echoing above the noise of screeching children, chattering parents and the thwack of someone playing squash in a court beneath us.

Stancer was in the bath when she heard the programme on the radio, recruiting women for the 1997 McVities Penguin Polar relay challenge to the North Pole. She had no Polar background other than through her grandfather, the Earl of Granville, who applied for Scott's ill-fated expedition to the South Pole and who was finally refused on the grounds that he was too tall to fit in the tent.

Fortunately, height restrictions were not enforced during the North Pole relay selection process or at 1.6 metres she may have been deemed too small to pull a sledge. There were to be five teams of four women in each team and as each team completed its leg another team was flown in to replace it. The selectors were faced with women such as Ann Daniels who had never had a rucksack on her back and Stancer who says she did not know the difference between a clothes peg and a tent peg. The trials were conducted on Dartmoor with SAS precision.

"At the end of the day it didn't matter if you crumpled and cried, as long as you picked yourself up. Fairly early on you have an intuitive feeling that you were going to make it into the teams. I think there is a destiny but I can't logically answer why. When I heard that they were selecting women I just knew with a dead certainty that I had to get into the team. I was going to be successful and I had a passion. I didn't know anything about the kit or how to hold a compass. We were sizing each other up as we were all from very different walks of life but we did have something in common, we were all completely useless amateurs!"

The twenty women were finally selected and each team successfully completed their leg, bunny hopping the 645 km from Resolute Bay to the North Pole, guided by an all woman duo, the American Matty McNair and the Canadian, Denise Martin. No amount of probing from me revealed anything other than a smooth ride for the teams, temperamentally anyway. As the women stepped onto the ice, the full cold blast of their weaknesses hit them.

"I learnt that I was very intolerant to what I thought were other people's weaknesses. I was rather startled to see weaknesses in me. I am a bit more tolerant now. I understand how a team works. It works with the team's strengths, not weaknesses and I have a much sharper intuitive sense of judgement."

Stancer went on to walk to the South Pole two years later with four other women from the McVities challenge. The team was unguided and reached the Pole with only one re-supply. Today, the women keep a polite silence as to team dynamics but by the time they reached the Pole, relationships were in tatters.

> "In Antarctica it is difficult to communicate although women are usually very good at it. It is very noisy because of the wind and you are travelling in single file for reasons of security, like the possibility of falling down a crevasse. You are wrapped up to the nines and when you break during the march, you only stop for five minutes. There is very little time for girly chit-chat. In the tent you do the repairs to your body and kit and do your communications and logistics, so it's not easy. I would say, to be honest, we were definitely divided"

Although she avoided divulging exactly how the team spirit among the five women unravelled, she appeared deeply affected by it. Yet, something even more painful happened and she looked genuinely anguished recalling it.

> "What actually hurt more is that I lost my log book with three-quarters of my account of the expedition. We had a re-supply three quarters of the way through the expedition. It was handed over to the pilots and they were busy having to juggle other teams and this precious logbook went missing. My record for my family and my son. It was very hard. When I think about it I still feel that I have been punished."

Stancer was determined to go back, but this time on her own and in 2003, sponsored by Snickers candy bar, she was back on the ice, walking solo to the South Pole.

> "I wanted to intensify the spirituality of the experience. Sometimes I was relieved to be on my own because no one could see how cack-handed I was! I knew that to do something unprecedented was important for motivation and no British woman had gone solo and unsupported."

A 40-year-old Norwegian woman, Liv Arnesen, had walked solo and unsupported to the Pole in 1994, the Norwegians yet again outstripping every other nation. However Stancer was not the only British woman chasing the North Pole that season. Leaving from Hercules Inlet at the same time was 37 year old Fiona Thornewill, seven years her junior.

As Stancer dragged her 120 kilo sledge into the face of the icy wind, she lost the Argos beacon, a satellite based tracking system, which was strapped to the back of her sledge. Most people would panic at being left without this vital piece of equipment, a devise that pinpoints position in case of an emergency. Not Stancer. She made a half-hearted attempt to look for it before setting off South again enjoying her new unfettered freedom.

> "I had a bad relationship with it and one day I turned around and it just wasn't there. I walked back for 20 minutes and it wasn't anywhere. I was pleased to get rid of the weight (2 kilos) and it was another thread cutting me off from the other world, from

the other reality. People at home panicked and I was threatened that I would be jeopardising the whole expedition if I didn't go back and look for it. It was a miracle that I found it as there was a ground storm going on. It took me 36 hours to cover 48 nautical miles which is another Polar record - the fastest person to go nowhere! I was initially driven by anger. How could I be so chained and shackled out here?"

Stancer's fear of failure and making a fool of herself far outweighed the physical fear. She says that that fear is all about the unknown.

"Get to know it and then it isn't so frightening"

What she hadn't bargained for was finding herself in a crevasse field in poor light. She opted to make camp for the night and secured her tent. Leaving the tent to 'spend a penny', a hole appeared in the snow. It suddenly dawned on her that she had parked her tent on a snow bridge.

"I discovered I was on top of a covered crevasse. If I moved and made a camp somewhere else, I might have found the same thing or fallen into a crevasse. I was in a field so I decided to lie low until the (light) contrast improved. I wriggled into my tent; it was cold but obviously I didn't light a stove. I put all my emergency stuff, my beacon etc., into my sleeping bag, and I slept! When I awoke, the light was good enough to see the path out. But I had to find something within myself to bolster my confidence up after that."

She hauled and skied, a little dot in the white wilderness, busying her mind with dinner parties and menus. Sometimes she came across the tracks of a Korean team heading for the Pole and, more worryingly, those of Thornewill.

After 44 days of slogging the domed American scientific base that dominates the South Pole came into view. She had made it but Thornewill had pipped her to the post by three days.

Stancer sidesteps the bitter disappointment that must have washed over her. Had she not turned back to look for the Argos beacon, who knows, she might have got there first. Finishing second on her solo attempt was a bitter pill but she says of Thornewill in a burst of laughter:

"She is a very good, genuine, Christian person and that makes it easier to swallow!"

Yet she experienced something that many other adventurers have described.

"When I got to the South Pole I remember feeling distinctly unexcited about it. I was knackered anyway. I wondered why I felt a fraud and I realized that anybody could do it and it didn't feel quite what I had anticipated."

In 2007 Stancer, with a 'deep urge to return to those parts' and with Mars Incorporated, the same company that had sponsored her previously under their Snickers brand, behind her, she set off to be the first woman to reach the North Pole solo.

Being related to the Royal family - the Queen Mother was her great aunt - and having Prince Charles as a sponsor would have certainly given her the edge on raising the sponsorship needed to tackle such a venture. She wasn't the first woman to make a solo attempt on the North Pole, but if she succeeded it would be hailed as one of the most extraordinary feats of bravery and endurance.

"You are a speck on five million square miles of ice. You don't feel small, you feel special to be there. You feel close to God or your Major. You start to shed your layer, your armour of social skills."

Ann Daniels, the gritty working class Yorkshire lass, was preparing for the same challenge for the second time and all bets were on her. Political wrangling between Russian and French logistic companies had blocked her first attempt two years earlier. She had already conquered the North Pole with a teammate five years earlier under appalling conditions. On paper she was tougher and more experienced than Stancer and she would leave no room for mistakes. However she was unable to raise sponsorship and had to drop out of the head-to-head.

Stancer had the clear run she needed but the Arctic conspired to thwart her every effort. Conditions were as cruel as anyone could remember and when drifting currents were not negating Stancer's meagre progress, she spent hours cutting through pressure ridges in order to drag her sledge forward. The storms were so violent that even Borneo, the Russian 'floating' base and runway which is built each year two degrees from the North Pole and caters for scientists and adventurers, broke up, forcing everyone to evacuate camp.

Several teams were on the ice heading for the Pole, including two highly experienced women, American Ann Bancroft and Norwegian Liv Arnesen, who was the first woman to reach the South Pole solo. Temperatures plummeted to -60°C. It wasn't looking good for Stancer. Within ten miles of setting off, two of her toes became frost bitten and if she were to continue it would mean certain amputation later. During her daily communiqué she received the news that Arnesen's toes were also frostbitten, not only on the same day but the same toes on the same foot. Arnesen and her American partner called it a day and aborted their expedition. The Arctic had its own agenda.

"Right that is it! That's the end of the expedition. How embarrassing, a premature ending! In fact it was for the Norwegian and American. I was aware that should I continue and should the infection spread up my foot, I was chancing something awful but I decided that I had a supply of antibiotics and an expedition doctor I could talk

to over the satellite phone. It was a very carefully calculated risk, and I decided to continue. I knew I would probably lose the toes, but I didn't mind about that."

It is argued that frostbite is the result of mismanagement and not simply bad luck, yet some of the greatest adventurers who feature in this book have suffered from it. It brought Borge Ousland's first attempt to cross Antarctica to a halt and as Rune Gjeldnes watched four of his toes turn black on his Antarctic traverse, he feared that his expedition would meet the same fate.

"Hands, to a degree, unless something happens and you have an accident, you can look after and you are aware of them, whereas your feet, you can't see them as they are in boots. I had no idea that day that they were getting frost bite until that evening when I was in the tent."

Lashing wind turned the ocean into a heaving mass of what Stancer described as 'ice junk'. Some days, wide tributaries of open water stretched in front of her, forcing her into her immersion suit to swim to the other side. On one occasion the hood of the suit slipped off her head and the suit began to fill with water.

"The dangerous bit was getting out and not turning into a human lollipop!"

Once back on solid ice she changed her socks and mitts and kept moving until she had warmed enough to set up her tent.

"When the ice was turning over and my little island was getting smaller, I ended up with nowhere to go. I thought it was going to roll over in the ice because there was so much activity in the water. I did put on my immersion suit. I thought if I got pitched into the water I might get crushed or I just might make it. It was terrifying but, I can't explain why, every morning I woke up with renewed hope that today would be better!"

Nature continued to rage with cataclysmic force. At times she could only make progress by jumping from one ice block to another, sometimes having to wait for two blocks to collide before leaping. Then her optimism ran out and she believed her final day had come.

"It was quite early on, among some very big pressure ridging. Temperatures had swung violently from -60°C to -40°C. It was even snowing. I thought this is not good. Suddenly ice started packing and moving and I found out later a whole large seam of pack ice had broken away from the land mass hundreds of miles away. I was caught up in the middle of this hell and maelstrom and the noise was overwhelming. I have never heard anything like it, or on that scale. All these walls of ice shooting up and crashing down, with black lines cracking up around me. I really had nowhere to run to with ice moving beneath my feet, so I pulled out my safety equipment, my satellite phone, a pair of bigger mitts and my puffa because I thought, if I am going to go in I will give myself as much time as possible. Then I thought 'what for?' To prolong a

cold and grisly death? There was no point in thinking about the emergency beacon because no-one was going to get there in time and no plane could land.
I pulled out my little picture painted by Jock which was laminated with a message from William on the other side, I laid it on top of one of the sledges and I focused on it, like a prayer, and everything receded. The noise and chaos, and even the fear, just seemed to back off. I became completely calm and completely ready to meet whatever was coming my way and I thought how strange, in the eye of death I am standing here thinking of love. It gave me this great light and this great calm."

As if by some divine intervention the ocean calmed enough for Stancer to set off again but the stomach churning eruptions continued every twenty minutes or so.

"I kept going though there were times of the day I just couldn't, so I would stand like a scared rabbit. But I got through the day."

All aspirations and dreams fallen, 89 miles short of the Pole

The days of endless scrambling, bashing through ice ridges and swimming across leads could take up to 15 hours a day. Stancer decided to change her routine to hauling for eight hours, sleeping for four, followed by hauling for another eight hours. The exhaustion must have been indescribable and, at times unable to stand, she was forced to make camp on her knees. She started to run low on painkillers and her frozen foot pounded with pain.

By the 75th day her mood plummeted, swamped with the anxiety of letting people down, particularly her son Jock, but she was damned if she was going to give up.

On the 84th day her re-supply plane was due. Gathering her strength she set about the stressful job of preparing a runway for it to land. It meant finding a flat pan, 305 metres of old, weight-bearing ice and clear of obstacles such as rubble or melt pools. Stancer struggled to find a landing area long enough. Finally the pilots agreed to land on less than 300 metres, just feasible by temporarily dumping some fuel drums they were carrying.

The plane landed safely and delivered the news that chilled Stancer's blood. The game was over. The pilots had reconnoitred her final push to the Pole and the Arctic Ocean was breaking up. Even if she had made it, they could not risk another landing to pick her up. She must board the plane and leave, then and there. All her months of training, her aspirations and dreams had fallen, 89 miles short of the Pole.

Flying in the extreme conditions of the Polar caps requires the best pilots in the world, usually Russian or Canadian. The safety of these 'bush pilots' as they carry out the hazardous 'pick ups' or drop re-supplies, lies partly in the hands of the adventurer who must prepare the runway.

Getting the plane in and out of the Pole of Inaccessibility was a monumental task. The flight involved a route over 2,500 kilometres without re-fuelling, so the plane was maxed out in fuel, therefore very, very heavy. We were at 3,725 meters elevation (add 20% elevation because of the high latitude) so in order to lift off Brian (chief pilot) requested a 5,000-foot long runway. With one shovel, we spent countless hours shovelling and stamping down a surface long enough to accommodate him. At 02h55 on Monday morning the plane touched down at the POI, the first time in over 40 years. One hour later, Brian revved up the engine to maximum RPM. We started moving down the runway, ever so slowly accelerating. It seemed to take forever before we finally lifted off the snow. A loud cheer erupted from all of us glued to the windows. All except for Brian who was focused on piloting the plane, as we were only half a meter above the surface. He kept the plane at this height for another several thousand feet as it picked up more speed before pulling the controls back and inching his way up. A few minutes later, he turned back towards us, a big grin on his face and gave us a thumbs-up.
A wave of relief swept through my entire body. We were airborne and on our way home. My responsibilities were over; my job done.

Paul Landry, guiding the expedition to the Pole of Inaccessibility 2006/2007

I had seen photographs of Stancer in the media after her return from her epic bid on the North Pole and was shocked at her frailty and drawn features as she leant on two crutches. I left it for several months before telephoning her. Much had yet to be healed.

"There will always be the same Rosie but I think something opened up in me that hadn't on previous expeditions. As you know, I have got into situations which were fairly frightening. This one - living with bowel loosening fear everyday - (in particular on a couple of occasions when I had done everything I could in the situation and had to wait for what I thought was certain death) does alter you.
There is not so much luck in reaching the South Pole because it's all about commitment, focus and endurance, whereas on something like the Arctic ice you may have all the ingredients for the recipe, but unfortunate luck. I am not saying I didn't reach the North Pole because of bad luck. A better person may have made it, but various elements conspired to throw every possible card against me. The ice cap will continue thinning. I had a micro-cycle within the greater cycle and for all the input I gave, it was sucked away."

It has been a difficult and frustrating return to normal life for Stancer. The goal that had focused her for two years has gone and nothing since, she admits, seemed very important, other than her family. Two toes have been amputated leaving her physically incapacitated while her foot heals.

> *"It's funny having a wound that is stitched up. When something has been removed from your body it has all sorts of strange after-effects. I wouldn't have thought it would have been such a big thing, for two such little things being removed. Your electronic defence system around your body goes a bit haywire. It upsets your balance and there is the sheer frustration of not being able to move around and multi-task; such as when you make a cup of coffee, you have to stand in the same spot to drink it."*

Several months later I attended a question-and-answer evening with Stancer at the Royal Geographic Society in London. She looked glamorous and appeared to have recovered much of her bright spirit. A photo slide of her taken shortly after she was lifted off the ice flickered on the enormous screen above her head. Staring out of the window of the Twin Otter were the beaten features of an old woman, eyes hollowed with hard labour and disappointment. All of that was now gone. She enthralled the lecture room which was filled to bursting with friends and supporters, including several members of the Royal family. She is right when she says:

> *"I have come back with something very valuable, a story everyone wants to hear."*

Most expeditions in the Arctic and Antarctic can be followed on the website, ExplorersWeb. Reports are transmitted directly from the adventurer by satellite phone or through the 'home team' as it was in Stancer's case. Often a spin is put on daily reports and they can be over-cooked to give dramatic effect. In Stancer's case the reverse happened. I don't believe we heard her voice. We did not gain a sense of the enormity of the task that lay ahead of her, the dangerous situation she found herself in and the sheer audacity and courage it took to carry on.

ExplorersWeb has its say too and it makes pointed observations. Often it is accused of being self-elected arbiters of Polar issues, which it denies, saying the 'rules' are collectively agreed upon by the Polar community itself. The British Polar contingent are rarely given a smooth ride by the website or, for that matter, by the rest of the Polar community. ExplorersWeb argues that Stancer invalidated her solo claim by making contact with people whilst receiving re-supplies.

Stancer already has plans for the future and she is dipping her toes, albeit a few less, into the water.

> *"I suppose if you cherish a dream you are prepared to work extremely hard in every sense; the preparations, the time and emotional input, as well as when you are on the ice the physical struggle and the psychological struggle. I can't imagine that if you have a dream you can't apply yourself one hundred percent."*

Web site: www.rosiestancer.co.uk

ERLING KAGGE

"The biggest challenge of a polar explorer is to get up in the morning."

There is a problem interviewing Erling Kagge: his record breaking Polar achievements are just one facet of a fascinating individual and to talk simply about his expeditions is missing the point of the Norwegian all together.

At the age of 20 he sailed across the Atlantic to the Caribbean, via West Africa, and back to Norway. He and fellow Norwegian Borge Ousland then went on to be the first to walk unassisted to the North Pole (a claim that has caused a major dispute) and he was the first person to walk alone and unassisted to the South Pole. A year later he climbed Everest and became the first person to bag all 'three' Poles (North, South and Everest). His expeditions have been part of a journey that has led him to become a lawyer, philosopher, highly successful publisher and a serious collector of contemporary art. He lives in Oslo with his partner, Jorunn, and their three small daughters.

I met the 1.9m Norwegian, who could be from central casting, with the physique of an athlete, a mop of blonde hair and startling blue eyes, at the offices, in the centre of Oslo, of his publishing company Kagge Forlag, which turns over 4.5 million euros a year.

Kagge's office looks as if it has been hit by a cyclone, with papers and books strewn on every available surface from desk to floor. It belies the nature of one of the finest Polar adventurers in recent times, who like all Norwegians, attributes his Polar successes to first-rate organisation. The thriving publishing company is responsible for 60 new titles a year and covers everything from Norwegian celebrity chefs to Norway's leading philosopher Arne Næss, with Joseph Conrad and Mark Twain in between.

Kagge's childhood growing up in a middle class Oslo suburb had a shaky start. He shunned all forms of authority as early on as kindergarten, from which he was expelled. He remembers his school days as a catalogue of horrors, of unforgiving teachers and a constant barrage of bullying for his awkwardness, poor speech, 'buck teeth and fat lips.' In spite of severe dyslexia he managed to escape into a world of fantasy and books. Being 'different', he believes, made him fight a bit harder.

In spite of his parents divorcing when he was 13 years old he remembers that he and his two older brothers had a fairly stable family life filled with endless ski and sailing trips, parties and concerts. No sooner had he finished his year of national service, than, at the age of twenty, he decided to live the dream and sail across the Atlantic to the Caribbean, via West Africa, and back with three friends, two, of whom had never sailed before. The photographs in Kagge's book, *Pole to Pole & Beyond,* are straight out of a Joseph Conrad novel. An azure sea; four young boys, nut brown and naked, fooling about for the camera on a small sailing boat that appears hardly capable of crossing the Atlantic.

There were times when their self-financed expedition was in grave peril as they were flung about in violent seas and water poured into the boat's open hatch. Yet there were many idyllic, sun blessed island-hopping days. The journey simply served to urge Kagge to seek more adventure. He went on to help crew a sailing boat across the Southern Ocean to Antarctica via South America.

Eventually the boy who couldn't pass an exam and threw his books at the wall with frustration turned into the man who acquired a legal degree, practised law for some time and spent a year at Cambridge University studying philosophy.

In 1990 at the age of 27 he set off on his first expedition, which catapulted him into the headlines. He and his fellow countryman, Borge Ousland, became the first men, or so they claim, to reach the North Pole unsupported.

The Britons, Ranulph Fiennes and Mike Stroud were striving for the same record the same year. They aborted their expedition 143 km from the Pole after a catalogue of mishaps, including running out of food. They believe, however, that they were justified to claim the 'furthest' unsupported trek to the North Pole, at that time.

The Norwegians originally set off with a third team-mate, Geir Randby. Nine days into the journey Randby dislocated a disc in his back when his 120 kilo sledge fell into a crevasse. He had to be airlifted off the ice. That, in Polar parlance, is considered 'supported' because the remaining men can then take advantage of the food and equipment belonging to the third man. It is as if a 'helper' has been brought along for some of the time.

Kagge and Ousland insist that all of Randby's gear went back with him except for two small pieces of communication equipment. More importantly, Kagge insists he and Fiennes

Face to face with a local

had a meeting prior to the start of their expeditions and they both agreed on what would amount to a 'supported' expedition.

> "At his office at the oil company he was working for we talked with Ran about what would be considered supported; for instance shooting and eating a polar bear. We did shoot a polar bear but we were so concerned about it we didn't eat it until we reached the North Pole. We agreed evacuation would be all right. It's bad sportsmanship to change your mind about the rules but on the other hand it is fair to say we started with three guys and one was taken off. I can see people have different opinions. I think Ran is a cool guy, but my point is he changed his mind. We did what we did and today it's not a big deal. "

So who makes the rules? Interestingly, Kagge disclosed at that time that Fiennes made the rules because he had made several attempts on the North Pole and he was considered 'the big man'.

Sniping aside, the Norwegians pulled off a magnificent 800 km trudge in 58 days, succeeding in what no man had done before. They became bone thin; their motivation was challenged daily by stretches of ink-black water or blockades of ice. Their progress was whittled away by counter currents and always the was the daily grind of the unspeakable cold.

Three years later Kagge set off to be the first person to walk solo and unsupported to the South Pole from the Filchner Ice Shelf and ironically, that same year, his two adversaries, Fiennes and Stroud, were setting off for an Antarctic traverse. Kagge was to cast another dark shadow on the British expedition. With extraordinary ease, considering the rigorous demands of the expedition, Kagge arrived at the South Pole nine days ahead of the British pair who had set out ten days before him. In his book *Shadows on the Wasteland* an angry Stroud describes Kagge as 'mean-spirited', claiming that Kagge had boasted of winning the race, when in fact they had all agreed previously there was to be no race.

> "Race? I do not remember whether it was mentioned between the three of us, but there was no doubt at the time that they were very eager to get to the Pole ahead of me and I wanted to get there before them. The press was of course more interested if a race was involved, although our primary goals were something else; they to cross Antarctica and I to get to the Pole solo and unsupported."

The two expeditions cannot be compared and need to be kept out of the same arena. Kagge was alone. He was not to have the luxury of companionship or someone else's helping hand but, on the other hand, his sledge was very much lighter than the Britons.

Walking to the South Pole was to be a rite of passage, a chance to experience the solitude he longed for. Yet he is not without ego or so pious that it was purely a search for enlightenment. He wanted to be the first man in history to walk to the South Pole alone without outside assistance and he wanted to get there before Ran Fiennes and Mike Stroud.

Determined not have any contact with the outside world and forbidden to leave the radio behind he dumped its batteries in the plane flying him to his start. He had saved weight by not only weighing his flimsy reading material, but also shaving his backside in order to limit himself to three rolls of lavatory paper for the journey. Every gram counted but it was ironic that he carried a heavy unusable radio for 1340 km. However he was determined not to leave any waste behind on his trek.

> "I took the radio but took out the batteries - it was a good move. To ski by yourself, you don't want to talk on the radio, it is a disadvantage. You talk to your loved ones and get news from home and it's very confusing. Borge (Ousland) talks on the radio every day. I think you must accept the circumstances. I didn't miss anything. I had the Argos (to send a signal) but I didn't have any communication. If I had known more about the expedition, I wouldn't have had the Argos. I wouldn't miss it at all but I didn't know that at the time."

It was an audacious challenge and no-one believed at that time that it was possible. He was told he was crazy. He arrived at the Pole in 49 days and 13 hours, in fine spirits, believing it was absolutely within his power to carry on past the South Pole and cross the continent because he felt so well. However he had not made the necessary preparations prior to leaving, so a traverse was out of the question.

In *Beyond the Limits* Fiennes writes, "Our Norwegian rival Kagge had altered his original plan to cross Antarctica to an attempt to reach the Pole solo and unsupported ......", suggesting Kagge had arrived at the Pole and realized to go further was foolhardy.

Result of the encounter

> "It was never ever the plan to cross the continent. It was not even mentioned at any stage. And I definitely did not have provisions with me for a crossing, there was no chance to just walk in and buy additional food and fuel at the South Pole base. This is something Ran and Mike started to talk about."

It is clear however that for Kagge, and probably for Fiennes and Stroud too, time has doused the inflammatory passions that have risen from pitching themselves against the harshest environments. Kagge adds, probably in a more condescending tone than a conciliatory one, 'despite the fact that they did not succeed, they did very well'.

As far north as we are now, only a couple of hundred kilometres from the North Pole, there is no nutritional basis for polar bears. Apart that is, from members of polar expeditions. We dive into our sledges and pull out our revolvers…the bear paces back and forth. It is an intelligent beast and we know that this is just its way of preparing an attack. By appearing uninterested it is hoping that we will not regard him as a threat. Borge wants to take a photograph but there is no film in his camera. He lays down his Magnum 44 handgun and loads his camera with a fresh roll of film. Then he gets me to pose between him and the bear.

The bear soon tires of this. It bows its head and stamps on the ice with its forepaws. I have never seen a bear make an attack before but I am in no doubt whatsoever as to what is about to happen. It's the bear or us.

The bear starts running. We have heard that a polar bear can attain speeds of 60 km per hour. Its body is swaying and it is 12 -13 metres away, coming towards us, not in a straight line but on a zig-zag course. Perhaps it has not made up its mind which one of us to go for.

Our handguns are cocked. I hold the butt of mine with both hands and when the beast is eight metres away we fire. Luckily we hit it in the chest.

The bear stops dead in its track, staggers and falls back a little. Then its bowels empty. Borge rushes forward to put it out of its misery. We cannot take the risk that we merely wounded it. The bear sinks down slowly on its knees and rolls over on to the eternal pack-ice. We are both relieved and sorrowful.

Pole to Pole and Beyond Erling Kagge

Kagge's expedition wasn't without frightening mishap. He jumped down a section of Frost Spur (a near-perpendicular ice fall) to retrieve some gear he had cached earlier to lighten his sledge while climbing up the ice fall. Expecting his feet to touch down on soft snow as he landed, he found himself dropping into a void and came to a halt straddling a snow bridge over a crevasse. He managed to wriggle himself free without disappearing into the void below. I wondered how he coped with fear?

> "You are not really frightened, like if someone was pulling a knife on you; you
> always feel afraid but you manage to suppress it. Even when we were attacked by
> a polar bear we were not frightened. You have to adapt to the circumstances. But
> afterwards you may be frightened."

Captain Scott and his brave companions endured appalling misery during their journey to the South Pole in 1912 only to find the Norwegian Amundsen had beaten them to it. To compound the horror of the journey all five men died on the way back but they are etched on the British psyche as heroes.

> "In Norway we don't have the expression 'heroic failure'. If you fail you are not a

hero. Ran is ill prepared in general but he has a huge willingness to suffer. What he lacks in preparation, he makes up in suffering. It is due to an English culture, they think they should suffer."

Having said that, Kagge believes the more you strive the more you get back.

"If it is too easy you don't get so much back, that is for sure. I think it should be tough. People can believe they are not supposed to have problems or have physical pain and they feel sorry for themselves. I think it's healthy to be able to accept that life is not supposed to be pain free, life is also about suffering. Military service may not be a good thing, but sleeping in the tent is a good thing and being cold for a few nights is good for self respect."

Kagge made up his mind, after a year at Cambridge University in England studying philosophy, that academia was not for him. Yet there is no doubt that, contrary to what his teachers believed, he is highly intelligent and a deep thinker. He has built up a significant art collection of Russian icons but mostly concentrates these days on contemporary art, visiting major art fairs both in Europe and the States each year.

"I am a very serious collector of contemporary art and I buy art and publish books for the same reason I was a polar explorer, I want to see what is over the hill. I have bought a piece a week for five to six years. Each year I change everything in my house. I lend to exhibitions and I rent a warehouse. I need to try and understand contemporary art. It's difficult to relate to. Damien Hirst? He bores me, he has gone down the drain, but he will come back."

Kagge is driven and restless He encapsulates everything of a free spirit. Since the age of 20 he has set himself impossible challenges and yet, against the odds, he has succeeded in so many fields. He needs challenges to feel alive and take from them 'the meaning of life.' A new dream is already forming in his head.

"It's more exciting in many ways being a Polar explorer than a publisher. There is a season for everything. I don't have the desire to keep doing the same thing again and again. Variety is good. Life has so much potential and

Made it!

*there are many things to do. I won't be a publisher for another 10 years but I have
my staff and I must see it through and then leave it to someone else."*

Kagge walks me to the train station before hurrying off to buy himself a wet suit to
accompany his newly acquired wind surfer. He suggests his next expedition won't be high
profile but he hints it will have something to do with sea, surfing and harnessing the wind,
though he is not exactly sure what it is yet.

He then looks at his watch and announces he also had a swimming lesson booked that
day to learn to do 'crawl.' Thinking I mishear him, I ask him to repeat himself.

"You know…(he demonstrates by swinging his arms over his head) crawl!"
I look at him utterly perplexed. He shrugs and then grins.
"I think everyone should know how to crawl."

Website: www.kagge.no
Books: Pole to Pole & Beyond
              Philosophy for Polar Explorers

DR VICTOR BOYARSKY

"It is not easy to go to the North Pole. It is quite expensive and it requires skill and even a short expedition is very hard. I have already led more than eighteen expeditions and I know how people feel. Most of them are suffering."

Russians understand ice better than anyone. Unlike with their space programme, Russia has remained transparent in their published results on Polar science and they are pre-eminent in the field of exploration. Their navigational skills in flying or sailing in icy conditions is unsurpassed and the majority of planes and ships to be found in the Arctic or Antarctic today are Russian owned and Russian piloted.

Victor Boyarsky, 53, is a radio glaciologist, explorer, head of the floating Borneo base and is in charge of Russia's State Museum of the Arctic and Antarctica in St Petersburg. His company, VICAAR, specialises in expeditions by ship, plane or on foot for tourists, adventurers and scientists in the Arctic.

I had arranged to meet the master of all things Polar in his hometown, St Petersburg, only to discover I had over looked the necessity of a visa. Not even Boyarsky, fixer extraordinaire, who can gain entry into the most testing Russian bureaucracy, had time to help me.

We arranged to meet a few days later in the German town of Friedrichshafen, where he was representing Red Fox, a Russian company, at an outdoor trade fair.

Boyarksy has spent half of his 33 years of married life in Polar regions, often away from his family for a year at a time. He worked as a scientist on the isolated and horribly bleak Vostok station in Antarctica where the lowest temperature of -89.3°C was recorded.

Boyarsky left for an epic crossing of Antarctica when his son, his only child, was a baby and he returned to find him running around.

The first thing that strikes you, as he strides across the foyer, is an impressive sandy coloured beard of hillbilly proportions, surrounding an equally impressive beaming grin. Boyarsky is turbo charged, his blue eyes dance with amusement and his self-taught English, spoken with a thick Russian accent, is a muddle of words ruptured by laughter.

Boyarsky is renowned for taking daily snow baths in sub zero temperatures and performing his daily bodily functions with lightening speed so that he is able to exit the tent naked. The need to struggle with layers of clothing in a freezing snow filled wind is not one of Boyarsky's problems. No one else has got it down to such a fine art.

We retreated into my overheated hotel room, and I watched with alarm as beads of sweat trickled off his forehead. He suggested we leave the door of the mini-bar open to try and cool things down.

Stepping out of an American Hercules I was enveloped in a hurricane of blown snow whipped up by the plane's propellers. Multiple layers of thermal wear couldn't stop the thin, cold, air grabbing my throat like a knife as I took laboured steps away from the plane. Behind me the Herc's engines would stay running for the one and a half hours it was on the ground to prevent them freezing. I jumped on the back of a battered Russian skidoo and bumped the short journey over a small rise to a collection of dilapidated huts, three quarters buried in snow. "Welcome to Vostok!" my anonymous driver shouted from behind his balaclava. It was high summer, and the temperature was -35 degrees.

If Antarctica is the Earth's final frontier, no outpost on this frontier is more final than Russia's legendary Vostok base. It resembles less an earthly settlement than how I imagine our first colony in space might be. More than a thousand kilometres from the coast in one direction, and another thousand kilometres to the South Pole in the other, it is as remote and hostile a spot as earth has to offer. In 1983 the coldest temperature ever recorded on earth - -89.3 degrees - was recorded here. Just 3 flights come into Vostok each year. Its only other connection with the outside world is an epic two-month overland tractor traverse from the Russian's coastal base at Mirny which brings in fuel. And yet Vostok has been more or less continuously occupied since it was established in 1957.

Jonathan Renouf. Producer of *"The Lost World of Lake Vostok"* BBC Horizon

His love of adventure sprang from reading Jack London books such as *The Call of the Wild* at school. He planned on following in his father's footsteps and joining the merchant navy but failed his medical so he continued his studies as a radio engineer. In 1973 Boyarsky landed the job as a radio glaciologist and radar scientist in the Polar regions. I wondered what this meant?

"It means that someone who is too lazy to study ice and snow by hand prefers to do it by remote sounding by radar. I designed a system which I put on an aeroplane and fly over Antarctica and the Arctic and check and measure ice thickness and make mapping. I really don't like too much glaciology because you have to work in thin gloves and check this and take samples and work with tiny things in cold weather which is not good fun."

His heart lies in the far northern Russian Arctic and in Siberia. He has witnessed how life has been sucked out of the northern settlements since the withdrawal of subsidies in post-Soviet Russia.

"Russians were really proud of their Polar achievements in the 40s, 50s and 60s because there was very big enthusiasm for Polar expeditions and science. There were huge, huge subsidies from government. These came down in 1999 because

of absence of management. It's not a question of money, even during the Second World War new stations were built; it's a question of management. Since 1999 it was decided that Russia did not need such a developed infrastructure for the North. They cut the supplies by big ships to all the small settlements. Where everything once worked, now it's dead."

His work included the complicated detection of 'neutrinos' which travel near to the speed of light and are able to pass through ordinary matter. Every second some 70 billion solar neutrinos pass through every square centimetre on earth that faces the sun. Antarctica, cold and with low electrical noise, and where the detection of electrical magnetic waves is easier, provides the perfect conditions.

In 1987 the programme was cancelled due to lack of money. It was a blow to Boyarsky but he set out to cross Greenland from South to North and following that, in 1989, came an invitation to join the first international expedition to cross the entire Antarctic continent via the South Pole by dog sledge.

The Transantarctic expedition, led by Will Steger, which included Geoff Somers, was the first crossing of Antarctica in one season. The team, including French and Japanese, covered a staggering 5,900 km and took seven months to complete.

"No one knows why they chose me because I cannot speak English, not at all. At least I could keep all Russian secrets to myself! They sent an official letter to the minister of foreign affairs asking for a Soviet member. No-one believed that it was going to happen, but my Institute offered me. I was very happy; not my wife, but she's used to it.

The Trans Antarctica was the biggest thing in my life. No-one could do it today with the restrictions of the dogs, the most efficient way of travelling. It was very special, we had such a good team and we still keep very close relations. The team was so balanced, too young is not good; it's not stable because the professional skills are not as valuable as skills of life experience. It's important to have mature people who don't destroy team spirit."

Boyarsky's Agency VICAAR monopolises the logistics of Arctic expeditions from Siberia, overseeing scientists, adventurers and tourists. Each year the company sets up a temporary base and runway approximately 89°N on drifting ice called 'Borneo' or sometimes 'Barneo'. It is an enormous feat that entails a 900 metre runway and a tented village able to accommodate 250 people. Each year it costs between 2.5 and 2.8 million euros to set up. Bad weather conditions and the breaking up of ice may mean sudden evacuation of all staff, personnel and equipment and being re-located to another ice flow, as happened in 2007 when 50-knot winds hit the base.

"The most difficult part is to build a runaway which will operate all months on a very far removed area like the North Pole. We don't have a stable platform there. We have breaking ice and we have to be ready to move everything out. Now we have professionals who air-drop our fuel, which saves a lot of thought and it's a

reliable way to bring enough fuel for operations. Before we used to bring the fuel by plane which is not efficient and very expensive. Now we make three drops in a row, maybe 40 tons, by parachutes. Secondly, we organise the runway to be accepted by Civil Aviation. It must be made in the proper way before any civil aeroplanes are let in. We keep two helicopters on standby, air crew and a big camp. The base cost 10,000 euros per person to cover expenses."

In 2005 Boyarsky's company came head-to-head in a conflict over permits with the French/Russian company Cerpolex who also supplied the logistics and air cover for expeditions leaving from Cape Arctichesky. Each accused the other of Mafia-style tactics and Boyarsky of sabotaging their outfit to gain control of logistics. Boyarksy retaliated with accusations of ineptitude and underhand dealing.

The exact truth as to what happened may never be known, but the result of the clash left three expeditions with annulled permits and they were taken off the ice. One of the victims was Ann Daniels, attempting the first solo female march to the Pole.

Tragically, a year earlier a young French-born woman, Dominick Arduin, drowned attempting the same record. Cerpolex, in charge of her logistics came under fire in the press for not organising a proper search and rescue effort. In the end her friends raised additional funds and Boyarsky carried out a further mission.

"Dominick's was an exceptional case but the company who did her logistics, a French company (Cerpolex), should have stopped her and not allowed her to go. If you take care of someone, you have to make sure first that they know what they are doing. You have to provide them with proper and correct information. Some people like to start from the shore and it is difficult to convince them otherwise but you have to be strong enough and not let them.
Polar travellers have to do the right thing; she tried to cross the area with suspicious ice. You have to wait for the ice to come in, or a big flow to lift you over."

Borneo floating Arctic Base

Boyarsky deployed two helicopters to scan a large area but there was no sign of the young French woman. It is believed Arduin took to her canoe and paddled across open water.

> "You cannot paddle thin ice. Sea ice -23°C degrees could be safe but the same ice with temperatures of -10 is not safe because of the salt. Salt makes ice absolutely different. Fresh ice even at three centimetres can hold you. Salt makes ice weak; at -20°C it's no good! You have to know where you are going in case it moves, you must have islands to jump on.
> I would have told Dominick. They tried to search for her but it was bad weather. Three weeks later I got a call from her friend from Finland. Could I organise one more flight search? This is expensive with two helicopters so I asked the pilots who were flying to Borneo. Actually Dominick paid the guys (Cerpolex) for her expedition and re-supply and they didn't spend the money."

More recently, in 2006, Boyarsky underpinned the rescue of the Swiss Thomas Ulrich who attempted to walk to the North Pole unsupported and alone from Cape Artichesky. Ulrich came within hours of losing his life in a terrifying ordeal.

During his second night on the ice he found himself in the middle of a raging storm that blew his equipment in all directions across the ice. The solid ocean beneath him started to break up as if made of fine glass. He left his tent and looked for safer ice but to no avail. The storm was turning the ocean into a juddering turmoil of broken ice. He made desperate calls to his camp manager, Hans, and to Boyarsky back in St Petersburg, who with his influence and expertise launched a helicopter rescue.

> "It was difficult to organise the rescue because I was in St Petersburg and the helicopter was 3000 km away. The weather was very bad. They refused to fly at night; the pilots were ready to fly but management wouldn't allow it. They said they can't risk ten people just to save one."

The terrified Ulrich spent two nights on the shrinking ice flow, in radio contact as Boyarsky bulldozed firstly the authorities to get the required permits to fly and secondly, the chief of the air company to mobilize the helicopters that would need to fly eight hours from Norilsk, the northernmost city in Siberia, to Sredniy and from there another 90 minutes to Cape Artichesky.

> "He spent two nights without sleeping. He was in touch with his wife and daughters and they talked. He was sitting in the middle of the ice and surrounded by the sea without a tent, no sleep, no fresh water. He told me he wanted to sleep and I said no Thomas, I will call you every 20 minutes! I called him from my home by radio. They took one hour thirty minutes to reach him from Sredniy. I called him and said they are on the way, as soon as you hear them, burn whatever you don't like, sleeping bag, make a fire so the pilots can spot you and they will from 20 km. I called him again, then nothing - no answer. Then two hours later the pilots told me they had him. "

As Boyarsky describes the rescue, in the darkness the pilots spotted Ulrich and banked away to return at a better angle. Ulrich, believing they were leaving him, panicked and shot off his flares and everything else he had at hand. The pilots joked he was trying to kill them. As they returned they hovered inches from the tiny ice flow that was keeping Ulrich alive. With the superhuman strength of a desperate man he leapt into the helicopter.

"When they came back he jumped straight up, straight inside. He was completely wet. They jumped out and picked up the sledge. Of course he was absolutely on the edge and he was lucky we picked him up. Two or three hours later there was a huge blizzard and he wouldn't have survived. There were 54 knot winds. I phoned the guy in Moscow who finally pushed for him to be picked up and I said you have saved the life of a guy and Switzerland and the whole of Europe has been watching. I am proud that he survived."

Boyarsky roars with laughter.

"Tommy (Ulrich) said to me, Victor if you are taking me out of here, I marry you!"

As the popularity for extreme adventure escalates, surely it is only a matter of time before an incident like this will end in another tragedy?

"We are offering three or five days just to get a feeling of what's out there and still survive. I don't think the market will increase. A realistic number is 200 to 300 people in a season. (Of which only approximately a tenth go on serious expeditions.) We never allow people without experience to go right away. If you have no experience you have to go to Borneo. You have to be able to pay for repatriation if needed and actually we can mobilize a helicopter in one or two days. If it's not something like a polar bear attack you can survive on the ice. It's not like water, you can keep yourself alive until the rescue."

In 1995, under the leadership of Steger again, Boyarsky set off on a 4,000 km dog sledge traverse of the Arctic Ocean. The team consisted of two younger men, a Dane and a Briton and to the disdain of Boyarsky, two women, an American and Japanese.

"Two young ladies, two young guys and two older men. I was sceptical. I was about to leave. I wanted to leave. It didn't make sense to be a part of women going across the Arctic Ocean. I had the feeling it makes it less, our incredible achievement. If you do something on the ice and suffer, I can't imagine women doing the same thing. I don't care about women doing their own thing in a women's team …but mixed …. I was afraid I was not strong enough to help the ladies in a difficult situation. I was completely wrong. I was traditional but they said forget it, we are team members, you don't have to care about us. In fact the girls were outstanding. I changed my mind, it is not the problem with the sex, it's the personalities."

The teams spent three years training for the expedition. However, on one of the training trials a year before setting out, team relations were already showing cracks. Boyarsky was questioning the imbalance of the team's dynamics and he was asked to try and make peace between them all.

> "In 1994 this Japanese lady wasn't a good skier and she fell and Will (Steger) wasn't paying attention and then he realized she is not there. She accused him of bad leadership. Both sides complained and they came to me and we made a compromise."

It was nothing compared to what followed on the expedition itself. Within three hours of setting off from Cape Arctichesky with the teams, dogs and sledges, all hell broke loose. Boyarsky was leading the way when he found himself on unstable ice.

> "We had three dog teams, 11 dogs each, and two people per team and then we started. We started too fast because the sea ice behaves absolutely differently to other expeditions. You have to look and make the right choice where to go. We started on 'fast ice,' I was in front, fast ice is okay, no problem, then as soon as we turned to the sea ice we find a good road.
> Unfortunately the lead dogs of the first team didn't follow me. I saw a big open lead. It was a very dangerous area and I turned back. The two lead dogs jumped onto a chunk of ice which is good enough to keep them up but nine other dogs between them and the sledge were in the water. We kept the sledge on the ice but it was -43° C. The nine dogs were tied from both ends and they had no possibility to swim, two dogs were completely under. I pulled the dog line out and there were two noses and at least they could breathe. Finally I cut the line with a knife and let the two dogs go, then all the others can swim. "

Eventually, the dogs were pulled onto thicker ice. I congratulated Boyarsky on his heroic actions and quick thinking in cutting the dog lines, which he dismissed immediately with the wave of a hand.

> "It takes five seconds. It's the only way, we had to loosen the dogs because they are tied. Unfortunately Steger also slips into the water. I skied back and also fell through the ice and I swim. I came to some ice and jumped out and tried to pull the dogs out that were under the water. I was luckier. I was in a one-piece suit, Gortex, completely zipped up. Steger was in a fleece and he become completely wet and as soon as we got out he turned completely to ice. We find a place to camp.
> Will (Steger) and I got pneumonia. We tried to continue but the others wanted to go back to the fast ice and we just followed. It took us two and half days to cover the distance which took us three hours before. We made camp and then got a blizzard for seven days."

At this point Boyarsky admits it was the most difficult moment of his expedition career.

The two young men had lost their nerve and one, the Dane, quit. Thinking the women would do the same, he and Steger were prepared to go it alone. The ladies were having none of it and steadfastly stuck to their decision to continue. The other man, the Briton, Martin Hignell, changed his mind and decided to stay but because of his earlier indecision Boyarsky never quite trusted him again. Two weeks later the team of five set off, but not from the coast of Arctichesky. They were flown to 88° N onto stable ice. They completed the incredible journey in four months.

Interestingly, Hignell went on to marry the American expedition member Julie Hanson.

Boyarsky is not a character particularly interested in breaking records. It would seem it is his geniality and knowledge of frozen places that have put him in the record books. It was impossible to imagine him going solo.

> "Solo? I don't like it, for me, one of the most attractive things being on expeditions is with nice friends to share experiences. I finished my big expedition in 1995 and started commercial trips. I always, always share my experiences with somebody and now I miss the situation to get together with people with the same Polar experience."

Boyarsky's energy and humour is infectious and I can't help thinking how much fun it would be to tackle either Pole with him.

> "I try to keep a positive feeling and I think if you can be good under regular conditions you can be good at extreme conditions. Optimist? Of course if you don't have the positive approach your life becomes more difficult, not only for you but for other people around because they start to see what is wrong and they also start to behave not correct. Some people say after reading my book that I make the expeditions look too easy and I am always joking around so people don't get the right feeling. If we describe the same day in our diaries it is a completely different picture. It looks like we are not in the same tent."

Who did he consider the great adventurers of today?

> "Borge (Ousland) is exceptional, very motivated, very professional and very well prepared. I am amazed by his achievements. Regular expeditions are difficult in daylight but this (North Pole expedition during the darkness of winter with Mike Horn) is special. Borge is exceptional and Mike Horn is more like me. Borge is too professional, too strict, too inside and Mike is more open, more similar to me, outgoing, very good with people."

Then he bursts out:

> "Ellen McCartney (round the world yachtswoman). I met her recently, brave lady! Richard Weber! Rheinold Messner (first person to climb Everest solo and without oxygen, and who traversed Antarctica in 1990) is my friend, my guru and my god!

Seventy per cent depends on skill and experience in the North Pole and there is a lot of space for luck for the ice conditions, ice drift and wind. It's challenging in terms of the unpredictability because you never know when you wake up. You lose your finger through lack of organisation. We get frostbite faces, not something that is serious. You have to behave right. It mostly happens with climbers because they have strict limitations on extra fuel and clothing. They can run out of fuel and they can't move. In Antarctica if you are strong you will almost sure be fine."

Finally, I wondered what he felt about the dire predictions of global warming.

"I am a bit suspicious because we don't have much winter here (in St Petersburg) but ice conditions are going up and down. Last year the weather was not usual in the North Pole, it was warmer, more windy and more cloudy but the ice was still good enough to cover the whole distance. A couple of years ago there was a lot of open water. I don't think things will change greatly that fast, but we will see."

I finished our meeting with the words

"Victor! I will have to go to the Arctic with you one day!"

Boyarsky hoots with laughter and I haven't got a clue what he means, but somehow, it doesn't seem to matter.

"Why not! You have to go otherwise it doesn't work!"

website: www.norpolex.com
Books: In Russian - translated as: -
             Seven Months of Infinity (Trans Antarctica)
             Greenland's Meridian (Trans Greenland)
             Everyone has his own Pole. (Poems)

SIR RANULPH FIENNES

"I definitely regret all the ones that failed."

There is something outlandish about the name Sir Ranulph Twisleton-Wykeham-Fiennes, 3rd Baronet OBE, which conjures up a picture of a starchy, aristocratic explorer of bygone days, rather more apt to finding himself in sticky situations.

It is true that Fiennes' Polar failures far outweigh his successes and it is difficult for anyone other than the British to embrace the swashbuckling 'Boys Own' school of adventure which can be best described as imaginative, gung ho and do or die.

Courage is a key component and the 64 year old Fiennes, who has been berated for lack of preparation by the Polar community cannot be accused of a lack of nerve.

His dismissal from the SAS (Special Air Service) for stealing gelignite to blow up a film set in an English village is well documented and reveals something of the spirit of Fiennes.

Looking back at his career as an adventurer, luck has played a crucial role in a catalogue of hair-raising near misses and narrow escapes, but so have fortitude and an extraordinary capacity to bear pain. He is described in the Guinness Book of Records as 'the world's greatest living explorer' for which he has been decorated with, amongst others, the Polar Medal with one bar. In the polar community he is respected for 'having a go.'

The Baronet prefers to be called by the simpler name of Ran. In his expeditions, whether in search of the lost city of Ubar in the Oman or tackling the turbulent waters of one of Canada's fastest flowing rivers, the Nahanni, in a rubber dinghy, or crossing the Jostedalsbre Glacier in Norway, he cuts a swashbuckling dash. He certainly has Hollywood looks for the job and was once screen tested for the part of James Bond.

I met Fiennes briefly at a lecture given by him at the Scott Polar Research Institute. The vast lecture hall was full to capacity and he generously gave the proceeds to the Friends of the Institute. Fiennes, like his third cousins, the actors Ralph and Joseph Fiennes, carries the actor gene. He is a skilled showman and the performance was slick, highly amusing and well rehearsed.

His second wife, Louise, hovered protectively around him and every so often they would exchange touches and glances. Fiennes lost his first wife, Ginny, his childhood sweetheart and expedition organiser, three years earlier. Here now was Fiennes with a second chance of happiness at the age of 63, with a pretty young wife and a baby daughter, who he politely informed me on the telephone he was not prepared to discuss.

I was only ever to meet him briefly that one evening. He was busy training for his imminent climb of the North face of the Eiger, which, for a non-alpinist and someone who suffers from vertigo, was an exceptionally brave challenge and one in which he succeeded. In spite of an introduction from a mutual acquaintance, I felt he would rather have me at the end of the telephone as, like all consummate self-publicists who have attracted bad press, Fiennes is guarded. There is little chance of him dropping his defence and none whatsoever of tapping into his emotional psyche. Fiennes is clear he doesn't do introspection.

When questioned by the psychiatrist, Dr Anthony Clare on the BBC radio programme 'In the Psychiatrist's Chair,' Clare described his interview with Fiennes as 'stirring a void with a teaspoon.' Yet the description of the untimely death of beloved Ginny in his book *Mad, Bad and Dangerous* is deeply moving.

I was to wait until he had returned from the Eiger when I was offered a telephone interview with a twenty-minute slot. It was going to be a bowl and bat interview. A colleague of mine said, "Don't let him intimidate you!" It hadn't crossed my mind until then.

Fiennes was born in Windsor, England in 1944 and never knew his father, who had died shortly before his birth. According to a friend of his, his three older sisters doted on him and, he suspects, thoroughly spoilt him, allowing him to get his own way. He spent his early childhood in South Africa and returned to England to attend Eton College, considered England's greatest school.

He followed his father's footsteps, joining the Royal Scots Greys and spent eight years as a non-regular officer with a stint in active service fighting Marxist terrorists in the Oman, which sharpened his survival instincts. Army regulations finally forced him to leave, equipped with not much more than 'trained in adventure.'

> "The best way was to do what we called adventure training, for which the taxpayer paid. We took the soldiers canoeing or skiing and when I became a civilian I needed to use that experience to make a living. That meant expeditions, which I am still doing in order to pay the bills."

Following a spectacular crossing of the Jotunheim glacier region of central Norway and the rivers of British Colombia, Canada, in 1979 Fiennes made his first sortie into Polar regions with the Transglobe expedition. The expedition circumnavigated the globe on its Polar axis by surface transport. It took seven years to organise and three years to complete and covered 56,000 kilometres following the Greenwich Meridian. Fiennes was accompanied by Charlie Burton and for part of the way, Oliver Shepard.

Fiennes raised £29 million worth of sponsorship including fuel, ship and ski plane. Six years into setting up the project he had a team of 25 people working full time, without pay. He and Ginny whipped up extraordinary loyalty, fired from their own commitment and passion and to this day Fiennes still manages to extract the same allegiance and support for his adventures. Anton Bowring who was responsible for finding the ship, the *Bengy B,* for the Transglobe expedition - "a huge mechanical beast that cost millions" - described Fiennes as "self centred in the best possible way, charismatic, very, very persuasive, who made you feel hellishly responsible once he gave you a job to do."

Shackleton's 1914-16 Imperial Transantarctic expedition took a year to organize and within weeks of leaving he had only raised half of the £70,000 needed. A last minute donation of £24,000 came from Sir James Caird, a Scottish millionaire. The placing of an advertisement in the Times asking for "Men wanted for hazardous journey, small wages, bitter cold long months of complete darkness, constant danger, safe return doubtful" is hearsay. However it is believed some 5,000 applications were received after the expedition was announced in a letter to the Times. He divided the letters of application into piles labelled Mad, Hopeless and Possible.

He was a leader loved and respected by his men for his humanity, equality and optimism, and was sometimes accused of 'fussing' too much over them. He based his selection on the men having "first, optimism: second, patience; third, physical endurance; fourth, idealism, fifth and last courage"

Fiennes pointed out that 25 years later no-one else had managed to go around the world on its polar axis by any route, so we were "the first and last". Whether anyone would want to is questionable. The South African adventurer Mike Horn circumnavigated the earth around the equator by foot, bicycle and canoe, unaided by motorised transport and the Briton, Jason Lewis completed a 13-year, 74,000 kilometre self-powered circumnavigation of the globe.

By 1990 few Polar 'firsts' were left to be conquered but one of the most coveted was to reach the North Pole unassisted. The Russian, Vladimir Chukov, had previously made two attempts, although details are sketchy. On both occasions team members died, one of a heart attack and another of a stomach complaint. Of the remaining team several had to be evacuated and those who were left finally made it to the Pole. The Russians conceded that their attempt had failed and the 'trophy' was still up for grabs.

Fiennes and his partner Mike Stroud had also failed on two earlier expeditions when setting out from the Canadian coast. As they prepared for their third attempt, this time from the Siberian coast, a piece of history was about to be repeated. A Norwegian team was preparing to reach the Pole from the Canadian coast. The two old Polar rivals, Norway and Britain, were once again pitched against each other, somewhat in the style of Scott and Amundsen: albeit this challenge was taking place at the opposite end of the globe.

In his book, *Beyond the Limits* Fiennes' account of his and Stroud's attempt describes a hellish march of blizzards, ulcerated blisters, failing eyesight, falling through the ice, starvation and finally running out of food 143 km miles south of the Pole. It was time to call in help and be taken off the ice.

The Norwegians, Erling Kagge, Geir Randby and Borge Ousland, were having a better time of it although Randby injured himself climbing over ice rubble and had to be evacuated. Ousland and Kagge continued and reached the Pole in 58 days claiming to be the first men to reach the Pole unsupported.

Fiennes and Stroud, understandably, were furious. They maintained that Randby's evacuation amounted to assistance and most would agree. Kagge refuted it implicitly at a showdown at the Royal Geographic Society claiming Randby's evacuation hadn't given them an advantage and the British were accused of sour grapes.

Fiennes' argument was that if Ousland and Kagge could claim they had reached the Pole unsupported regardless of evacuations, then so could Chukov, in which case Chukov would have been the first man to reach the North Pole unsupported; and he had a point.

> "We point out if losing one of your party en route and having him picked up by a ski plane does not compromise you then they (Ousland and Kagge) did get to the North Pole unsupported. So did the Russians under Vladimir Chukov. The furthest north they reached that year was the point at which the third man was removed. We got further than that so we broke the world record that year by a long way - so we are very happy with that."

The more hard-bitten adventurers I talked to view Fiennes' and Stroud's expedition as failed and question why it should be in the limelight at all.

Fiennes description of his North Pole push with Stroud in *Beyond the Limits* makes thrilling reading. Seven days into the expedition his ski binding broke. In order to save weight, the men had not taken spare bindings and Fiennes had no option but to wade through deep snow, a slow and exhausting process. They discarded their gun for the same reason, which gave them little comfort when they discovered fresh polar bear tracks. In spite of warnings from an eye surgeon to protect his ailing eyes from bright sunlight, Fiennes removed his goggles and eventually his sight became too bad to navigate.

Stroud took a dip in the ocean up to his neck which nearly cost him his life and they fell through the ice many more times after that. By the time they were rescued, with their rations gone, they had lost 14 kilos each in weight.

Fellow adventurers accuse Fiennes of an absurd lack of preparation for his expeditions. To strap snippets of foam cut from a mattress on his blistered heels may seem ingenious to some, but to most professional Polar adventures the practice of strapping feet with medical tape prior to long marches is normal practise.

Danger and suffering makes adventure writing more interesting and it is often tempting to 'turn the colour up' when describing the wretchedness of expeditions. Presuming Fiennes, who is an excellent writer, tells it how it is, then his expeditions are a monument to adversity. What is indisputable is his ability to take punishment and his capacity to tolerate discomfort and pain.

"Well that is just luck, it is genetic."

Fiennes makes it clear that he is bad at any form of introspection, philosophy or hypothesis but that he has turned to religion during expeditions and when things have become particularly bad he has turned his thoughts to his father and grandfather, neither of whom he knew.

"But I respected both of them greatly and I sort of imagine them looking at me and I don't want to do anything that would make them resent (me)"

Fiennes had attempted only two solo expeditions: the 2000 traverse of the Arctic (aborted due to frost bite) and the 1996 traverse of Antarctica (aborted due to kidney stones). I was interested in what he thought made a good solo adventurer?

"Because I am not a good solo traveller, I don't really know - total self confidence I would imagine."

And a good travelling companion?

"Anyone who is prepared to listen."

In 1992 he and his teammate Mike Stroud put themselves through hell to be the first to man-haul and use sails where possible to cross Antarctica without support. The Antarctic is

clamped by two ice shelves, the enormous Filchner-Ronne ice shelf, a mini continent of 430,000 square kilometres of ice attached to the main continent and the even bigger Ross Ice Shelf. A 'true' traverse takes in the crossing of both ice shelves

It was a huge undertaking and the sledges alone, crammed with food and equipment to last them three months, weighed a massive 220 kilos each. It is the beast of man-hauling. The more you haul, the more calories you burn, the more food you need, and the more weight you must haul.

Fiennes's old adversary, Erling Kagge, left from the same spot ten days later, setting his sights on an exceptional prize: to be the first person to walk to the South Pole alone and unsupported.

Terrifying incidents in crevasse fields, punishing days of extreme exertion and short tempers finally found the two Britons at the South Pole 68 days from setting off. Kagge had arrived ten days earlier and in good shape.

Fiennes and Stroud were wasted. Stroud had lost 18 kilos in weight and Fiennes 23, yet they were only half way through their ordeal. They gathered the little strength they had left and continued.

Suffering from hypothermia and bone infections, bloodied, blistered and raw, they ploughed on day after day. They lashed each other with harsh words and doctored their wounds. Their rations were pitifully small and the cold and starvation were slowly grinding them down. For Stroud, besides the personal achievement, the expedition was a scientific exercise to collect medical data on diet and physical stress and despite Fiennes' propensity to faint on seeing needles, Stroud took blood and urine samples throughout.

To reach the Ross Ice Shelf it is necessary to descend the famous Beardmore Glacier, discovered by Shackleton in 1908. It is a swathe of fissured ice 160 km long and sometimes 48 km wide that cuts through the Transantarctic Mountains and onto the ice shelf.

"There was a constant worry that the white-out would come down before we got off it, and also we were very, very cold indeed, much colder than we had ever been before or ever been since, which might point to a mistake which happened on day one."

Fiennes was referring to the dumping of some of their warm clothing to lighten their sledge loads.

The men finally stepped off the continent and onto the ice shelf. They had crossed Antarctica from the Atlantic to the Pacific oceans. It was Stroud's wish to continue to McMurdo, believing they still had a small chance of completing the full crossing but Fiennes believed it was too risky. They had shot their bolt. They had not achieved what they had set out to do, but it was the longest unsupported journey, 2170 km across the white continent.

Much has been documented about the slanging matches between Fiennes and his teammate during the expedition. Many of the clashes related to accusing the other of holding up progress and, on one occasion with Stroud crippled with diarrhoea, Fiennes suggested that on arriving at the South Pole Stroud could retire and he would carry on alone. Stroud was incensed at Fiennes' callousness and reminded him that he had waited for Fiennes 'for the best part of two months as he did his stupid plod behind me.' Fiennes apologised but Stroud wrote in his book *Shadows on the Wasteland*, 'I had seen a side him I didn't like one bit.'

However, as a measure of the regard in which Fiennes holds Stroud, he says:

> *"To this day the only person I would want to go with on any expedition with would be Mike Stroud. Admittedly, on one of them, which was the crossing of the Antarctic continent, we both wrote books afterwards which made the most of any bits where we would not speak to each other or had nasty thoughts about each other in our heads and both of us made the best of that but we immediately made it clear to the journalists who tried to overdo it, that we liked each other very much indeed and that we would do expeditions again in the future, which we have."*

Throughout Polar history the privations of expeditions have brought out the very best and the very worst in people. There are partners in modern day Polar journeys whose co-dependency has succeeded in pulling off unparalleled successes, as in the Canadian Richard Weber's and Russian Mikail Malakhov's unsupported walk to the North Pole and back, the Norwegian, Borge Ousland and South African Mike Horn's walk to the North Pole in winter and the two Norwegians, Rune Gjeldnes and Torry Larsen's unsupported traverse of the Arctic. All talk openly about the band of brotherhood. Throughout Polar history even the strongest bonds have shown cracks in extreme times of adversity.

> *"I have been worse today and scarce able to walk along in my harness, so have not been much assistance. The medicine doc is giving me makes me so fearfully sleepy, I have quite a struggle to keep awake on the march. We are 24 miles from our next depot by dead reckoning.*
> *Shackleton privately forced upon me his one breakfast biscuit, and would have given me another tonight had I allowed him. I do not suppose that anyone else in the world can thoroughly realize how much generosity and sympathy was shown by this: I do, and by God I shall never forget it. Thousands of pounds would not have bought that one biscuit."*
>
> Frank Wild's diary Nimrod Expedition 1907-1909

There are many examples of acts of human kindness such as the well-recorded one by Shackleton.

Equally, during the four months Shackleton's men were stranded on Elephant Island in such terrible conditions, a pledge of silence was agreed amongst the men on their release and it is only now, nearly a hundred years later with the publishing of journals kept at the time, that we learn the lengths men would go to in the times of desperation.

According to *Elephant Island and Beyond* by John Thomson,* Thomas Orde Lees was the least popular member of Shackleton's men stranded on Elephant Island. A pessimist and

*Published by the Erskine Press 2003

complainer who had the habit of squirreling away his rations, it is said he was targeted to be the first man killed if the men had to resort to cannibalism. His daughter recalled that her father had told her about a ballot among members as to who would be the first for the 'cook pot'. His name was drawn, and he believed he would have been killed if Shackleton had not returned to Elephant Island.

During the early part of the expedition when Fiennes and Stroud were still on the Filchner Ice Shelf a terrifying phenomena of apocalyptic proportions occurred which they respectively describe in their books *Beyond the Limits* and *Shadows on the Wasteland*. Finding themselves in a crevasse field, without warning the snow bridges covering the crevasses began to explode with a deafening boom. The bridges collapsed into the bottomless holes beneath them throwing clouds of fine snow into the air.

The men were surrounded by gaping fissures, not knowing if the ice beneath them might implode at any moment. A crevasse burst open between them but miraculously not under them. Attached by a safety rope, which under the terrifying circumstances was of little use, Stroud at one point found himself gawping into a crevasse 14 metres wide and 36 metres long. It was as if the ice shelf had been gripped in some surreal Indiana Jones episode. It was extraordinarily lucky that the men made it to safer ice that evening.

I asked Fiennes if he could explain why these phenomena should happen and he suggested I talk to Dr Charles Swithinbank, a leading glaciologist. Charles wrote: 'I read Ran's description and also Mike Stroud's. Things must have been most unpleasant, but I do find over-dramatization and insufficient clarity in both their descriptions. Unfortunately Ran selected about the worst possible route, not the one that I had advised him to take. I advised both Kagge and Ousland, and neither of them had a problem in this area.'

There was more than enough drama in the expedition without having to exaggerate this episode. From a scientific viewpoint there is no explanation and more information is needed. Perhaps Antarctica has not yet divulged all its secrets.

By 1996 there were very few Polar 'firsts' left to be conquered. One however, was the crossing of Antarctica, not just unsupported but solo. Fiennes was to rise again like a phoenix out of the ashes. He was not alone. His old adversary, Borge Ousland, threw down the gauntlet the same year, as did the Polish adventurer Marik Kaminski.

Tensions ran high as Ousland and Fiennes were holed up in Punta Arenas in Chile waiting for the weather to improve. Fiennes was well aware that the unfathomable Norwegian had honed his preparation to perfection and the para-wing that Ousland would use for the crossing made his own 'sail' look like something from the Flintstones.

Ousland commented that Ran Fiennes's biggest problem is 'he can't learn from his mistakes'. In his book *Alone across Antarctica* he says Fiennes 'was no chicken' and commanded respect; nonetheless 'all his expeditions bear the hallmark of having been ill prepared and unduly laborious as a result. There is no question as to his pluck, but the whole foundation is wrong when suffering is elevated to an aim in itself, rather than trying to make difficulties as negotiable as possible.'

Ousland tried to persuade Fiennes to set off through the safer and less arduous route of the Dufet Mountains but Fiennes chose the Frost Spur which, on seeing it for the first time, was met with 'disbelief and apprehension' as a wall of crevassed ice loomed in front of him. I wondered why he hadn't followed Ousland's advice.

"I listened to Borge and I listened to Marik. I listened to both of them very carefully and I decided with my particular sledge load it would be much more sensible (to go) the better-known route, which was Frost Spur. So Marik Kaminski gave me great detailed descriptions on how to get up the Frost Spur and gave me diagrams. So I followed his advice. Someone can say with retrospect I would have been better off following Ousland's advice than that of Kaminski but I respected both of them."

To get all his gear to the top of the Spur, Fiennes had to relay it up bit by bit. It took six ascents in appalling weather with only a single two-inch spike underneath each boot and a twelve-inch screw hammer tacking him to the glacier. With grim tenacity, Fiennes succeeded.

Many adventurers use the strategy of breaking things down into small manageable goals in order to keep going; a 'one day at a time' approach for even much shorter targets, possibly not looking beyond the next tea break.

"I had to do that a couple of months ago on the north face of the Eiger because it took five days to get up it, all of which was unpleasant and to try and look up at what was still rearing above was a very, very bad idea. But I couldn't look down because of the fear of vertigo and I definitely had to compartmentalise."

He believed he was truly in with a chance of making it across the continent although unlikely to beat Ousland, but, four weeks into the expedition, he found himself throwing up and writhing in pain with a kidney stone blocking his urinary tract. No amount of painkillers could relieve the agony and there was nothing for it but to release his emergency beacon and ask for evacuation.

Ousland with his state of the art para-wing, swept his way across the continent smashing all records.

Fiennes was to make one more attack on a Polar 'first'. In 2000 he set out to be the first man to ski and haul a sledge solo and unassisted from the Canadian coast.

Ousland had successfully done just that six years earlier, but from Cape Artichesky on the Siberian side. With two sledges weighing a combined 231 kilos Fiennes set out, relaying his sledges over the jumble of pressure ridges. Not far from the coast a broken sledge forced his return to Ward Hunt Island for repairs, which he successfully completed and once again he set off across the unstable ocean ice.

He progressed for the next 10 hours before disaster struck. Harnessed to his small sledge he stepped onto an ice slab which suddenly tilted, throwing him off balance and onto his back. The sledge carrying his communication gear, food and fuel, slid into the water and although it didn't sink completely, the harness ropes became caught under the ice. He flung off an outer mitt and plunged his hand into the icy water to release the snagged ropes and providentially the sledge rose to the surface. With the sledge back on the ice he replaced his mitt but the damage was done; his hand turned waxy white with frostbite.

Heroically, Fiennes made the painful five-hour journey back to the coast and contacted his base manager who arranged evacuation by Twin Otter the following day. Thus Fiennes' fourth attempt to reach the North Pole was scuppered.

Much has been recorded of him truncating his blackened fingers with a fret saw in his garden shed. The treatment of frostbite is a long, painful business. The pain during the 'defrosting' period is excruciating and continues to be so as the affected part blisters, blackens and scabs. The sensation is described as similar to receiving electric shocks. It can take months for the demarcation (separation) of dead and living tissue, during which time high doses of antibiotics stave off infection. Amputation is deferred as long as possible giving healthy tissue time to grow.

Fiennes grew impatient with the pain and discomfort and he took it upon himself to amputate the tips of his fingers. I suggested cutting off his own fingers was a good way to attract publicity.

> "Most good journalists like to be nasty in a cynical way. They go for what they consider is the jugular and they say people are egoists and they only do things like cutting off their fingers to get publicity. Anything you say will not prevent them putting in that snide angle. I cut my fingers off, as Beyond the Limits should make absolutely clear, to avoid a lot of pain and a lot of expense, so that answers that one. If you don't get publicity for the sponsors of your expedition, whether it's photos of their logo or anything else, then you won't get sponsored on the next expedition nearly as easily; well QED - you must get publicity if you want to make a living."

In his career Fiennes has raised millions for charities but one suspects that is not his driving force. His well written books and beautifully presented talks have afforded him a good living but his extraordinary facility for self promotion is what sets him apart. The title 'the world's greatest living explorer' is a title envied and ridiculed in equal parts by many of the adventurers I spoke to but ask just about anyone for the name of an explorer and they will come up with that of Ranulph Fiennes.

Books include: Mad Bad and Dangerous to Know: The Autobiography
Fit for Life
Living Dangerously
Beyond the Limits - The Lessons Learned from a Lifetime's Adventures
Captain Scott
To the Ends of the Earth: The Transglobe Expedition
Mind over Matter
Bothie the Polar Dog

DR MIKE STROUD OBE

"You are in a very strange position because the more you eat the better you feel the stronger you remain and the heavier your sledge will be, the slower you will go, the more food you will need. You have this impossible calculation that you are guessing at."

Perhaps because of his 'day job' as senior lecturer in Medicine and Nutrition and Consultant Gastroenterologist at Southampton University Hospital in the south of England, Stroud has no need to throw himself into the limelight of adventure.

Neither, I suspect, is it in his nature to do so. He is known largely as Ranulph Fiennes's expedition partner but has remained in the background, despite his considerable achievements.

He was the doctor on 'In the Footsteps of Scott', an expedition lead by Robert Swan in 1984-6 and he took part in four or five attempts, he cannot remember how many, on the North Pole with Fiennes. He received an OBE and the Polar Medal for the first unsupported crossing of Antarctica in 1992 and ran seven marathons in seven days on seven continents, partnered again with Fiennes.

Stroud grew up in the South of England with his two sisters and attributes his love of the outdoors to his father taking him hill walking as a young boy. It was after a trekking holiday to the Himalayas that he decided to become a doctor to give him the opportunity to travel.He qualified in 1979 and became a member of the Royal College of Physicians in 1984.

"As far as the expeditions are concerned I do them primarily as an adventurer and the fact that I am a doctor as well gives me more opportunities to do research on them which makes them even more interesting. I am not doing the expeditions as a doctor but because I like doing them."

In the introduction to his book *Shadows on the Wasteland* Stroud describes his misgivings before meeting the tall, military, gregarious Fiennes, and noted the disappointment etched on Fiennes's face as he shook hands with this extremely short, unassuming man who was about to man-haul with him to the North Pole. Yet, it wasn't long before Stroud was charmed by Fiennes, charmed enough to continue partnering him on many other expeditions.

Descriptions of Fiennes 'the world's greatest living explorer' oscillate between charming, arrogant, masochistic, self-centred, loyal and dogmatic. Naturally, the interest lies in having Stroud divulge the 'inner workings' of Fiennes, a man people either love or love to hate. Yet the person who knows Fiennes better than most revealed little. That is until each man wrote his own account of the Antarctic traverse in 1992 and every journalist's prayer was answered. In *Shadows on the Wasteland*, when the chips were down, Stroud wrote of his wish to kill Fiennes. In Fiennes's book *Mind Over Matter*, Fiennes wrote he and Stroud had grown to hate each other.

Today, of course, the past vitriol is put down to the hellish demands of the expedition. It would be naïve to think that during the brief telephone calls I had with both men anything new might be revealed, although Stroud is certainly less guarded than his fellow adventurer.

> *"As I said in my book, I don't believe Ran's report of how he feels or why he does things. They don't really hold together. He is actually adamant that why he does things (expeditions) is because he can't do anything else. It is just a load of rubbish. He clearly likes doing it or he wouldn't have got into it in the first place. He certainly wouldn't have kept going because he is perfectly well off and doesn't have to work at these things. He is very, very keen on being perceived as being the leader and decision maker but when you actually travel with him he is perfectly prepared to listen to things."*

The Antarctic traverse was at the time the longest unsupported walk ever undertaken, some 2,173 km, but was it was incomplete in so far as the two men had set out to cross the continent from the Filchner ice shelf to McMurdo, 2,845 km which was bagged by the Norwegian, Borge Ousland in 1996.

Stroud agonised at to whether they could have continued, in spite of the terrible state they found themselves in. There is enormous satisfaction in completing a challenge but that is not always enough reason to put yourself through continuing hardship. Ego is a trait he would rather be without but was it his ego that suffered in not seeing the project through?

> *"I have thought about it a lot. I don't dismiss it's an element. The fact that we hadn't done everything I wanted to do remained very important to me. I have met other adventurers who have pretty major ego problems. I hope I don't have them on the same scale. Opportunities to go to these places and obviously to push yourself are quite interesting things to do.*
> *That's what I like about our walk across the Antarctic; no-one had ever tried it because it wasn't possible and clearly it was. Since using good kites it has been bettered. I was told that when we did that walk Reinhold Messner (the greatest climber and first person to summit Everest without oxygen) said 'they must be lying, they cannot have done that' and I have taken that as the highest possible compliment. He did a supported walk across. It was not meant as a compliment but I took it as one."*

Stroud has never attempted a solo expedition.

> *"I would be hopeless. I don't think I'm someone who would function well alone. In a sense I would lose one of the powerful motivators of not giving up, that is, losing face immediately with someone else or letting them down. I suspect I would give up rather quickly if I was on my own, although in some ways I think it would*

*be rather interesting to find out. I did go up Mt Erebus on my own when I was
doing the Footsteps of Scott (1984) and that was quite an interesting experience in
a huge storm on the mountain side and no tent."*

Stroud has had his fair share of crashing through the ice on the Arctic Ocean and falling down a crevasse in Antarctica. Had Fiennes not found him struggling to stay afloat, as the weight of his rucksack dragged him down into the cold black depths of the ocean, he would have been lost. The sides of the crack he fell through were too high to haul himself out. The pain of the cold water felt like a tight band around his chest and his muscles ceased to work. Yet refusing to succumb to blind panic he managed to swim to a narrower part of the chasm and inch himself out while holding on to Fiennes's ski-stick. It was a close call.

*"Either of those things are pretty frightening but you don't have a great deal of time
to think about it, at that moment. The most frightening thing to ever happen to me
was to be avalanched in the Alps. Enough came down to carry me and one other
down a very long way and you have enough time in an avalanche to think about
death. I suppose you have enough time in the Arctic Ocean. I also saw that the
avalanche was going to take us over a very big cliff; it didn't, but I thought death
was inevitable."*

Failure plays an important part in Polar travel. It ups your game for the next attempt. There are simply too many challenges to conquer to expect to succeed on a first. The majority of extreme adventurers only succeeded having served their apprenticeship of failure and only then are they able to push out the boundaries, to go beyond the accepted capabilities of human endurance.

In many instances the fear of failure is what drives one forward and those who can clearly differentiate between irrational fear, as in fear of the dark or being alone, and rational fear, as in falling through the ice or polar bear attacks, make the best adventurers.

Stroud dismisses the idea that luck plays a small part in Polar adventure. The risks are minimal 'as long as you know what you are doing'. Both Fiennes and Stroud have been accused of being ill-prepared for their expeditions, mostly by the Norwegians.

*"I would defend that we are not well-prepared. Look at his (Fiennes) record. It's a
little harsh to be critical."*

During the post-expedition media flurry, Fiennes would not admit to his weaknesses during their journey; in fact he was quick to point out Stroud's inadequacies. Stroud quietly seethed, as he believed he was the stronger of the two, but, for all that, he believes Fiennes is not of a malicious nature but simply driven 'to make a good story.'

*"These places do have some inherent dangers but nevertheless I would consider
getting into real difficulty is bad luck. There may be all sorts of reasons you might
not be able to walk across Antarctica but dying is not high on the list. If you are
going to climb K2 then you would be pretty stupid to ignore the figures which*

make it blatantly obvious that there is a fair chance you may die. I wouldn't say that there's a lot of luck in surviving these things but I do think that explorers' accounts can be a little misleading."

It is generally accepted that you need to consume 6,500 calories a day whilst sledge hauling. The conundrum for unsupported journeys is to balance the amount of food that needs to be consumed with the amount that has to be hauled. The introduction of kites has meant that distances can be covered more quickly and therefore less food needs to be carried, making loads lighter.

"Calories can't change in weight; all you can do for food is alter the proportion of fat, protein and carbohydrate and remove water and make them dry. There is a limit to that technology, so the concept of food that weighs nothing and yet gives you everything you need, is obviously scientifically impossible. So it hasn't changed at all. The only thing you can do is make judgements."

The only time during our conversation that the mild-mannered Englishman became heated was the mention of a television programme about the television presenter Jeremy Clarkson driving a 4x4 to the 'North Pole'.

"Jeremy Clarkson! Complete prat! Environmental ignorance! The Magnetic Pole is just somewhere in North Canada but to claim it is immensely difficult to drive there, is just ridiculous! They have huge vehicles that regularly cross that area on the ice. It was just a fatuous claim! You could do it in a Mini let alone in a special vehicle, it's nothing like the North Pole, it's just a joke!
The same as the relays of the first women's team to get to the North Pole, that is a stupid concept - they did sections of it."

Stroud's accomplishments in adventure go far beyond Polar regions. For example he led the UK team in the gruelling Marathon des Sables. His medical reputation in the field of endurance, nutrition and survival is dazzling and he has worked as an advisor for both the British army and the RAF. His lectures are slick and entertaining. Yet it is difficult to creep from under the shadow of Fiennes who does not relinquish the role of controller with ease.

When I asked Fiennes by email if I could have Stroud's address he answered, 'Mike Stroud is very very hectic at present. He might be able to answer a few very specific queries. Would you like to send them to me and I can pass them on to him. He may or may not be able to respond (if he is in the UK)'

With little trouble I contacted Stroud directly who was more than happy to answer my questions. Fiennes need not fear, Stroud seems to genuinely mean it when he says,

"He is a very, very good travelling companion."

Books: Shadows on the wasteland
           Survival of the Fittest

RICHARD WEBER

*"The North Pole. It's tougher than
climbing Everest, no question.
I would say that even the
South Pole is harder than Everest."*

The best Polar adventurers are invariably the best skiers and none comes better than the Canadian Richard Weber, who began skiing in 1961 at the age of two and went on to represent Canada in the cross-country World Championships on four occasions.

He has completed six full North Pole expeditions - more than anyone else in history - and the 'firsts' just keep rolling in. First Canadian to reach the North Pole, first person to reach the North Pole from both sides of the Arctic Ocean, first person to trek to the North Pole using snowshoes exclusively and, the one expedition that may never be repeated, the first unsupported expedition to the North Pole and back to land.

I met up with Weber in Ottawa in yet another noisy café, grateful that the quiet Canadian who shies away from publicity had taken the time to drive in from Gatineau Park, near Chelsea, Quebec where he lives with his wife Josée Auclair and their two sons, Tessum and Nansen.

Tall, slim and although balding looks much younger than his late forties, he answered my questions in a quiet voice but with short, rapid fire eye-to-eye contact, not wavering for a second.

Interestingly, Weber has never attempted the South Pole. He is the king of the Arctic, with the record of an unsupported march to the North Pole and back that he, with the Russian Mikhail Malakhov, pulled off in 1995.

He and Malakhov, a thoracic surgeon, were the first to suggest taking tourists to the North Pole in 1989 to walk the last degree. It was a hard sell says Weber; people 'couldn't get their head around it'. Today, several companies and many guides offer the opportunity and it is becoming a well trodden path. These days Weber will only guide complete expeditions and if you want to have one of the greatest Polar heavyweights to accompany you, it will cost something in the region of a quarter of a million Canadian dollars. And he is not short of work.

He also runs the company Arctic Watch with his wife, guiding and taking people on Arctic adventure trips to his lodge on Somerset Island in Nunavut, where they can watch foxes, musk ox and Arctic birds and Beluga whales gathering.

I was firstly interested in talking to him about his 2006 expedition to the North Pole guiding Conrad Dickinson. Dickinson was the first person I, starry eyed and ignorant, interviewed for the book.

The two men wore only snowshoes for the entire journey, the first time it had been done, foregoing the safety of weight spreading skis or moving at a faster pace. There was less than three inches of ice underfoot and one could easily plunge into ocean, which they both did.

> *"To go there unsupported is still a serious undertaking; it's very demanding. We had been trying snowshoes for years on our North Pole dashes (last degree) and for someone who can't ski they are much, much better. On skis you can reach out and feel the ice. Salt water ice doesn't snap, it flexes, but with snowshoes you take a step and you are committed. They were good at the beginning; at the end they cost us on flatter ice. It was more difficult for me because I am a better skier than Conrad. Tons of Brits who haven't skied end up breaking equipment!"*

Dickinson described the snowshoes as pastry cutters, which was well demonstrated when Weber, who had never fallen through the ice before, dropped into the freezing water up to his armpits.

> *"I wasn't scared when I fell in, I was pissed off with myself. I rolled in snow and shovelled it over myself to soak up the water. Everyone says you should change your clothes and it was below -30°C but the water isn't that cold - just about freezing, so I thought I am just going to keep going. I knew one time of a Russian falling in and he hadn't the chance to change his clothes so he kept going, they are really tough. I didn't change my socks and boots and my feet got cold."*

Weber, who has had 20 years experience on the ice, is the perfect person to pronounce on climate change in the Arctic. His first expedition to the North Pole was as far back as 1986 with an international team led by Will Steger and a team of 21 dogs.

> *"The arctic was very different to '86. We had navigated with the sun the whole way and I remember the ice eight to ten feet thick; you could see it, looking down a crack. When you got pressure on the pans it buckled and a blue line of monster ridges would come out of the horizon and you had to try and find a way to get the dog teams across. The last expedition (with Conrad Dickinson) was warmer and foggy. The ice was so thin the pans just crumple up instead of breaking up around the edges and you get huge areas of just rubble. We couldn't figure it out; we were drifting west and we should have been drifting south east. I was very surprised but the scientists said the currents had changed. I don't ski towards the Pole, I ski 15 degrees to the left of the Pole taking the drift into account."*

Weber and Malakhov's 1995 march from the Canadian coast to the North Pole and back without re-supplies is without doubt one of the most daring Polar expeditions in modern history.

They had attempted the same expedition three years earlier with two other team mates; one who decided not to start, and the other who also turned on his heels and headed for home 39 days into the punishing journey.

Their first attempt was fraught with problems, with the pilots informing the adventurers they would not launch a rescue after a certain date due to weather conditions. Pressure piled on the men to move as fast as they could to the Pole, turn around and head back to Ward Hunt Island. If the expedition necessitated a pick up, the further south they got on the return trek the cheaper it would be. However, every exhausting kilometre fought northwards, was mostly wiped away by negative drift. At times it was as if they were literally standing still. On the 57th day on the ice they nearly lost everything.

Death in the Arctic

In late April in 2001 the Japanese adventurer, Hyoichi Kohno, set out from the North Pole on an extraordinary 5,000 km odyssey to ski, walk and kayak across Northern Canada, Alaska and Russia, to finally arrive in Japan. He called the expedition 'Reaching Home' and estimated it would take him six years to complete.
Approximately 700 km from the North Pole his radio signal fell silent and a search party left the Canadian coast by plane to look for him. His abandoned sledge, one ski and one pole were spotted from the sky, a mere 100 km off the North Coast of Ellesmere Island. It took two days and two further attempts before the weather allowed the Twin Otter to land. The pilot, Ross Michelin, found the Japanese's frozen body beneath thin ice, tangled in rope that was still attached to his sledge. It looked like Kohno had fallen into a lead and was unable to pull himself out.
Kohno was an experienced adventurer. He was the first Japanese to reach the North Pole solo, four years earlier. He had walked from Los Angeles to New York, crossed 5,000 km of the Sahara desert pulling a cart and climbed Mount Aconcagua, the highest peak in South America and the 6,194 metre Mount McKinley in Alaska. However Kohno's final expedition was beset with problems. He suffered severe frostbite only five days into the trip, forcing an evacuation. After a month's delay he was flown back onto the ice. This alone could have contributed to his tragic end.

What at first appeared to be an ordinary lead on closer inspection turned out to be a 'river' of flowing ice that 'would churn and somersault chaotically around like clothes in a washing machine'. Malevolent and silent, it swirled, and gathered pace, catapulting shards of ice out of the water and then just as quickly it would subside before erupting again.

The men stood on a pressure ridge and were so mesmerised at this spectacle they dropped their rucksacks and ventured forward to take a closer look. Suddenly, they found themselves standing on a piece of moving ice that was being swept along with the current, separating them from their critical backpacks and sledges. They ripped off their skis and hopped from one small piece of ice to another before they found themselves back on the 'bank' and finally re-united with their gear. They could do nothing but sit and wait and watch.

Several hours later they tried to cross the 'river' again and were once more balancing on a tiny ice flow in the grip of the current which carried them helplessly into the path of a loose pressure ridge the size of a small ship, heading in their direction. There was nothing for it but to brace themselves for the collision. The horrendous impact smashed the ice floe they were standing on in two and they struggled to remain upright as the shattered ice flow tilted, threatening to throw them into the maelstrom. It was as good as over for the brave men.

Unbelievably, the ice platform on which they stood became hooked in front of the wayward pressure ridge as it continued its forward journey. They were literally being shunted along with the rest of the frozen debris. As they brushed past a moving pan, its surface standing half a metre above them, Malakhov saw a means of escape. He hauled himself and his two sledges up on to it and immediately lent over to help Weber. Within seconds of heaving his partner up onto the shelf, the small ice flow that had sustained them for the terrifying ride, was swallowed up by a whirlpool; they had come to within a blink of going under.

Weber, in his matter-of-fact manner, was not going to dwell on having witnessed Nature at its most chilling.

"It was the most dangerous moment I have ever spent on the ice. Falling into the ice is not such an issue when there are two of you but if it hadn't killed us we would have lost all our gear. I have seen other frozen areas like that but we hit it when it was moving and it went on and on for hours."

They continued to fight a punishing daily duel with the ocean and finally were within 39 km of the Pole but their only chance of making it back to land meant they must turn back. They calculated that if they could cover 28 km a day they would reach Ward Hunt Island in 24 days. After that they would run out of food

On the 89th day on the ice they could hardly believe their ears and their eyes, a spectacular yet alarming drama was unfolding before them. First, the familiar sound of a "blow" then two whales surfaced in a lead. Hitherto, no whales had been spotted in the middle of the Arctic Ocean. It was June 20th. The men had been on the ice for more than three months and the vice like grip of the Arctic winter was weakening rapidly. It was time to put an end to their misery.

The plane was called in and the adventurers sat back and gorged on the food they had left; rationing was over. They prepared a landing strip and awaited the pick up; already the possibility of attempting the impossible again was ticking over in their heads.

Two and a half years later, finally raising the $200,000 sponsorship needed for the challenge, the two men set off again. This time they left on the 14th February, during the murky light of the Polar winter, more than a month earlier than the previous expedition.

They left half their provisions at Ward Hunt Island and shuttled and relayed the rest further north, making sure they marked their passage with small black flags and GPS readings. They set up what they hoped was a Polar bear proof depot and then headed back on a fourteen day journey to Ward Hunt Island to collect the rest of their supplies. It was a terrible risk to take. It would be easy to lose their provisions on the drifting ice in the vastness of the Arctic or have them disappear into a fresh lead and sink to the bottom of the ocean.

Weber struck me as exceptionally down to earth; rational, someone who would not spend too much time communing with God or Arctic phantoms. Yet like many adventurers he experienced something that caught him off guard. As he set off back to Ward Hunt Island he was convinced he was being accompanied by a 'third presence.' He was quite clear as to its benevolence and intention to play a supportive role and he looked forward to each time it reappeared. Describing the phenomenon was one of the few times he became animated during our conversation.

"The 'third presence' was weird. I am not a particularly spiritual person and I said 'okay, what is this?' I didn't have a clue. It was absolutely a presence. I talked to Misha about it and he didn't sense it. The first time I realized it we were coming back from a depot trip and we were looking for our old camp. We lost the trail and Misha was looking one side and I was looking the other and I thought I don't have to look over there, the other person is looking for me. I had a strong sense. Just before we got to the North Pole we left our tent and stuff on the ice and skied the last three miles to the Pole. It was like 'snap!' it was back with me, 'Okay! Now guys I am joining you for the last bit, this could be fun!' It was so strong, I didn't even say to Misha it is back, that seemed rude. It happened early on when we weren't tired, so it wasn't through stress but it hasn't happened again."

On reaching Ward Hunt Island the temperature fell to -58°C but they could not delay their return to the depot for long. They gathered the rest of their belongings and headed out onto the ice. Arriving at one of their black marker flags they checked its coordinate and discovered the drift had moved the flag 2.8 km eastwards.

Finally, they found their cache and they were now set on their journey to the North Pole.

For the next 47 days the Arctic threw everything it could at them, miserable days and better days, treacherous snow, drifting and snow blindness, but like automatons they marched, slept, ate and marched again.

Finally on 12th May, after 81 days on the ice, they arrived at the North Pole. There was no inclination to rejoice. Exhausted, they made a U turn and set their sights on the return journey, a 740 km bone-crushing march back to Ward Hunt Island. Only then would they allow themselves the luxury of celebrating.

On June 15th Weber and Malakhov arrived back at their starting point, the first men in history to reach the North Pole and back without being resupplied. They crawled into their sleeping bags, hardly able to move. It had taken them more than three and a half months to complete one of the greatest Polar journeys of modern time.

There is no doubt that the Weber and Malakhov combination made the expedition successful. As Weber said, Malakhov had the 'bits' he didn't have.

"We didn't have any real arguments. He is a doctor and I am an engineer. I like organising the trip, putting it together, that is what I do, I am a details guy and Misha is big picture. He came up with stuff like how do you digest 7,000 calories because you don't have enough enzymes in your stomach to digest all the fat. (They took tablets.) We were on the edge but we weren't starving and we didn't lose a lot of weight."

Weber on the great Peary debate

That expedition with Matty (McNair) and (Tom) Avery was good marketing but it didn't prove a damn thing. They made the same average number of days and no-one is arguing about that, they are arguing about the last bit. Avery didn't even do the speed Peary did, even for one day and on top of that Peary did it 1909. Today Avery should be able to do it twice as fast. We can do ten times better today, we are fitter, stronger, better equipped, better educated. The fact that he (Avery) struggled even to make the same time, then take away the GPS, take the away the SAT 'phone and the nylon runners on the sledge and put on steel. We are arguing the speed to the Pole. Try going from Ellesmere to the Pole with only a compass - you would never get there.

Reading Weber's book *Polar Attack* you get a sense that he would rather not have radio contact with the outside world when out on the ice. For some, focusing on the daily demands of the expedition then, at the end of the day, having to make contact with what may as well be another planet, is an intrusive bind. If things went really wrong a rescue party might not reach you in time anyway.

With Thomas Ulrich, he believed he was about to be crushed and sunk by a ferocious Arctic Ocean and his radio was his life-line as he hung onto the comforting words of Victor Boyarsky back in St Petersburg, and he was rescued in time. With the pressure of sponsors, family, insurance and base teams, to forgo 'phones and radios is not a choice these days.

"You can't worry about the house or the family. There is nothing you can do. It's better not to have communication. I hated it; it took you into another world and it takes a lot of time and energy. It slows up the expedition. It makes it safer, especially in the Arctic but to die up there is stupid. Dominick (Arduin) took off on her own in a kayak; you can't kayak up there. The Japanese guy was by himself and it looks like he was trying to save his gear. Of course solo is more dangerous."

"It's a tragic mistake to die in the Arctic. I have done some dumb things a number of times but a single mistake is not going to kill you. I have seen lots of stupid mistakes that people get away with when they should have died.
One group was doing the 'last degree' to the Pole and they got to about ten miles of the Pole to a camp where they were going to be picked up. They left everything there, including their radio and skied up to the Pole. They were so exhausted they couldn't ski back. It just so happened a Russian helicopter came along and took them back. We had the ice river but we were stupid to have ventured into it."

Everyone has a polar bear story and, not surprisingly, Weber says he has seen some 50 bears during his years of Arctic travel but the chances of running into them on the Arctic

Ocean is small and the chances of running into an aggressive one is even smaller. Some just happen to be more persistent than others.

> *"We had a bear in the kitchen two or three times a night for 10 days. We got stuck out of the camp due to weather and there was a mother, two cubs and two single bears. Our place was just trashed. They all went away except for one single bear and someone said that bear is going to cause trouble. I could have shot it but I didn't have a permit. For days that damn bear would come back into camp. We slept with a gun. One night Josée ran into him in the dark and he growled and she growled back even louder and the bear backed down!"*

Unlike Peary, towards the end of the expedition Weber and Malakhov shot a seal, part of which they devoured with relish. Remembering Borge Ousland's determination not to eat the meat of the Polar bear he dispatched on his way to the North Pole, in case it labelled his expedition as 'supported', I wondered if Weber hadn't had the same misgivings? He smiled as if remembering the delights of the feast.

> *" It was delicious. No, you make your own rules."*

Web site: www.canadianarcticholidays.ca
Books: Polar Attack

DR MIKHAIL MALAKHOV

"To do an expedition where every step has to be calculated, you need to know a lot about nature, about ice, about the human body and yourself. It doesn't just come with a physical condition it comes with a total life experience."

The name Mikhail (Misha) Malakhov, one of Russia's greatest Polar adventurers, surfaced in many Polar conversations, yet I am ashamed to say I hadn't managed to pin him down. But finally I was able to speak to him on the telephone and it wasn't long before I realized that it was an oversight of mine not to have been more tenacious.

Malakhov, a thoracic surgeon and former politician, had served as a physician on a Soviet Antarctic base. He came to the notice in the Polar community in 1988 when he took part in the Soviet-Canadian *Polar Bridge* expedition. The thirteen-man expedition, which included Richard Weber, left from the Russian side and successfully crossed the Arctic Ocean with supplies either flown in or dropped down by parachute. Prior to that Malakhov was part of the 1986 Soviet Polar Night Expedition, a 740 km ski in complete darkness, lighting their way by nothing more than hand held torches.

He joined Robert Swan's *Ice Walk* expedition in 1989, followed by one of the most remarkable expeditions of modern times, an unsupported march to the North Pole and back without resupply, again with Richard Weber.

With excitement and rising anticipation at speaking to the famed Russian I asked him what had been his most recent expedition? He answered proudly, in well-spoken English with a beautiful Dr Zhivago accent that he had recently organised a tennis game at the North Pole. I had to ask him to repeat his answer.

"Yes, I did a small trip to the North Pole and I arranged a tennis game. I am using tennis to keep myself in good physical fitness and this is the 100th anniversary of the Russian Tennis Federation. You know Russian tennis players are very good and as a present for the Federation I organised a tennis match at the North Pole. We took racquets and balls and made a tennis court and we did it."

The 'team' was made up of Russian businessmen and a politician from Ryazan, the region where Malakhov lives. It took three hours to mark out the court and adjust the net and they played three sets! Because of the drift they covered 200 km on skis. It wasn't a trip for the faint-hearted but Malakhov was keen to return to the Artic for a 'breath of fresh air.' He is planning another 10-day trip to the Borneo base on the Arctic next year for another tennis tournament.

Malakhov was 33 years old when he set off on *Polar Bridge*, the Soviet-Canadian expedition. His English was negligible but for him it was a chance to embrace an exciting new culture.

> *"There were eight people from different countries and I am from a socialist*
> *country. For me it was not a trip to the North Pole, it was a trip for understanding,*
> *a discovery of western people. It was more interesting to me than Arctic ice*
> *because I saw the Arctic ice in a previous expedition and I knew what it was, but*
> *other people from another system, that was very exciting for me."*

There was one expedition I particularly wanted to talk about, the legendary North Pole haul and back without resupplies. A march from the coast to the North Pole in itself is considered an extraordinary feat: without support or resupplies is beyond most peoples' grasp. It took Weber and Malakhov 108 days, the longest unsupported polar journey on foot and on skis in modern history. Yet Malakhov brushed off any suggestion of heroism. However I challenged him by saying no-one since has attempted the same expedition.

> *"It will be repeated but it will be already the second expedition! Why not! People*
> *have better equipment and food and people always want to improve on*
> *something that was done before. I am surprised that after 12 years no-one has*
> *tried to do it - I would like to say it was too difficult and we did a great expedition,*
> *but to be honest, I didn't find an answer for myself. Looking back we can't find*
> *we made many mistakes but it was a huge experience. We spent more than one*
> *year with drifting ice on the Arctic Ocean as our base. It's not about just being*
> *strong, it's not enough."*

I pressed the point that the Arctic Ocean today, according to other adventurers, has more open water and therefore has many more challenges.

> *"There are ways to cross all this open water - there is suit and sledges - your*
> *movement can still be quite straight. Of course conditions for skiers are different*
> *but not more difficult.*
> *There are ways we can overcome all these obstacles. I have crossed the ocean*
> *when we have had more water than in 1995. These are not obstacles for people*
> *who really want to do Polar expeditions, it is just lack of experience."*

Another expedition to have serious obstacles was that of Borge Ousland and Mike Horn travelling to the North Pole during the Polar night, again considered 'a first' at that time.

> *"The point is that I have travelled through Polar night. What is Polar night? When*
> *they started it was dark, when they finished there was sun and before that it was*
> *twilight. Twilight is light, it means it's not in complete darkness."*

Perhaps then he may rate the more recent expedition undertaken during the Arctic winter

by the two young Russians, Matvey Schparo and Boris Smolin? I suggested to Malakhov that Arctic travel is in the psyche of Russians, but he disagreed.

"I consulted for them. They left one month earlier (than Horn and Ousland) but again they arrived middle of March. They had two and a half weeks of very good twilight. I don't want to say bad things, but Polar explorers have to tell the truth. One day people will recognise that some haven't been honest. Now it is happening with Peary and Cook. It's more difficult to travel in darkness but if you are prepared for it with good lamps it becomes reasonable."

As described in the chapter on Richard Weber, and in his book, *Polar Attack*, written with Malakhov, the two men had a terrifying experience on their first attempt to make it to the North Pole and back. They were swept along in a thrashing ice 'river' which threatened to plunge them into the ocean. I had heard Weber's account, but what of Malakhov's memories of that day?

"It wasn't the most frightening experience of my life but it was still very dangerous and you don't very often have such conditions in the Arctic Ocean. You need to do something or you will be dead. That's all. It was horrible, definitely. If your remember I said (in the book) 'It must stop, it must stop!' It was like an intuition, everything would be alright. It would be illogical to stop all our efforts because of a huge piece of ice."

Yet, it was touch or go whether they would escape with their lives.

"But at that moment you are thinking about what you should do, which piece of ice you should jump on and when everything stopped for a few seconds, it was our chance and we realized it. If we had been paralysed we couldn't act. It was a memorable situation. I had the same situation in Antarctica when a huge block of

*ice started to move towards us on the ship. I said it must stop and it stopped!
Twelve years later in a similar situation in the Arctic I said the ice must stop and it
stopped!"*

I tried to envisage this tower of ice that came towards him in the Antarctic. The boat,
20 metres high, was dwarfed by the 50 metre high ice- berg bearing down on them.

Another incident I was keen to put to Malakhov was the 'third presence' Weber felt on
their expedition. Malakhov did not sense it.

*"Conditions are so unusual. It sounds strange but when you are there, in unusual
conditions, it's not strange. A body can react differently than when you are in
warm conditions. As a doctor I was interested to watch this unusual reaction. For
me it's clear, during the polar night expeditions you have very strange visions and
hallucinations, your brain creates pictures from other life experiences because
there are no bright moments. Day after day there are no colours, only black, and
you need to have colours. It's just a sensation to keep you normal. For Richard it
was a normal reaction for the human body in unusual circumstances. Don't forget
Richard has had a technical education and I have had a medical education. I need
to find an explanation for feelings but if you ask who will repair our stuff he will do
it much better than me. That is why we were a very good team. We both brought
something to the common table: Richard with a western education and me, with a
socialistic education, who had got used to surviving in much harder conditions.
This combination was very successful. This project was just for the two of us."*

BØRGE OUSLAND

*"Time ceases to exist; you become more like an
animal, completely naked, relying on instincts…
That happens after a couple of months being alone.
All the layers are peeled off, you are down to the core
and are just like a stone age man."*

The crushing disappointment felt by Captain Robert Falcon Scott on discovering Amundsen had reached the South Pole a month earlier resonates through every Briton attempting Polar records today. The reputation that Norwegians rule the ice is as true now as it was then. In all of my research there is one name that has commanded near iconic reverence and that is of Borge Ousland. No wonder. He has crossed 6,000 km of the Arctic Ocean and 4,000 km of the Antarctic, much of it solo.

I met the 1.9 metre fair-haired, laconic Norwegian, fittingly, in the Grand Hotel, which had honoured Roald Amundsen with a banquet in 1912 on his heroic return as the first man to reach the South Pole. Ousland dismounted his bicycle and suggested we talk in the hotel's coffee bar, where he knocked back two apple juices and a coffee, complaining of dehydration after his run that morning.

Self-assured with an air of nonchalance, he manages somehow to be detached and at the same time immensely engaging. Some questions, those you feel he has been asked a hundred times before, are answered in a low monotone, the words momentarily suppressed in a sigh. In fact he sighs frequently, which is disconcerting, yet he has a twinkle in his eye and he laughs easily.

He grew up and has remained in the Oslo area. His childhood was fun, stable and filled with family outdoor pursuits with his brother and two sisters. He has a teenage son, Max with his former long-term girlfriend Wenche and has recently fathered a baby daughter.

At the age of twenty-two he became a saturation diver, which entailed spending days and sometimes weeks at a time at the bottom of the ocean working on oil-rigs. I enquired as to why he would choose such a dreadful job and he retorted in mock frustration 'because it was an adventure!'

By the time he started his mandatory military service with the Norwegian elite Special Naval Force, he had already skied across the Greenland Ice Cap from the east to west coast accompanied by two friends.

In 1990, with compatriot Erling Kagge, Ousland completed the first trek to the North Pole from Ellesmere Island in Canada, without support, or so they claim. It is true they did not receive re-supplies, but a third team-mate was air lifted off the ice following an accident. According to the 'rule book' the rescuing of a team member invalidates the claim of an expedition being 'unsupported.' It caused a bitter dispute with Sir Ranulph Fiennes and

Dr Mike Stroud who were also marching towards the Pole, but from the direction of Siberia.

The Britons were forced to abandon their gruelling journey 143 km short, due to lack of food but at least they could console themselves with having reached the furthest northerly point unsupported. To have that record plundered possibly unjustly by the two Norwegians was more than they could bear.

Norway has produced the greatest explorers in Polar history: Roald Amundsen, (1872-1928), the first man to reach the South Pole; Fridtjof Nansen, (1861-1930) explorer, scientist, artist, author and Nobel Peace Prize winner (1922), the first man to cross Greenland and who survived against all odds with his partner Fredrik Hjalmar Johansen, a journey that spanned three years across the Arctic; Johansen himself (1867-1913), the most experienced Polar explorer on Amundsen's South Pole expedition and Otto Sverdrup (1854-1930), who captained Nansen's ship Fram and later explored and mapped a total of 260,000 square km of the Canadian archipelago.

Some time later, a heated clash rebounded off the hallowed walls of the Royal Geographical Society in London between Kagge and Stroud. To rub salt into the Britons' wounds the press accused them of sour grapes. Ousland is unrepentant.

"It didn't change anything with regards the weight of the sledge because Erling and I had the same weight all the time. The thing that happened didn't affect us in a positive way; it actually affected us in a negative way because the airlift took three days: that was three days of food. We just made it in 58 days and we only had food for 60 days. We felt it was a fair way to do it and we are more concerned with the adventure of it. If you break everything down, you can say the GPS (Global Positioning System) is support and swimming across open water is support because you use a suit. So I have pulled back from those discussions. I do my trips the way I want to do them."

Four years later, in 1994, Ousland established himself as the Polar supremo by setting off solo and unsupported to the North Pole from Cape Arctichesky, on the western Siberian coast.

Cape Arctichesky, often the starting point for North Pole attempts, is an inhospitable spit of land surrounded by seething sea ice, the last post of terra firma before stepping onto the frozen ocean.

"It's like being in the trenches of the Somme in the First World War. You get the order that tomorrow morning you are going to get out of the trenches and attack and you know that those German machine guns are going to most likely wipe you out; that's the feeling you have the night before you go.
Arctichesky is a terrible place - it's like hell. I shiver when I hear that name. I think it is because it is the end of the world, the last piece of land before the Arctic Ocean starts. It's shallow water, ice moves around it, crushing, opening and

closing, ripping things apart. It can just open up under you. You are vulnerable,
like jumping on a carousel moving at full speed. Sometimes there are 20 metres
of water and it closes up. It's moving so fast, once you jump there is no going
back, you can't go back. When you start you are in the maelstrom."

On the Siberian side, as opposed to the Canadian side, currents pull the ice away from the landmass, creating channels of open water between frozen ocean and land. It is not unusual for adventurers to be delivered by helicopter on to stable ice further north, missing out the treacherous coast line altogether and giving them a better chance of reaching the Pole. To add to the danger it is where you will most likely come face to face with polar bears. However, to claim a 'clean' record, it is necessary to leave from a land mass either from the Canadian or Russian (Siberian) side.

"That is why it is so horrible. You leave everything behind; it's like walking through
an invisible wall. Everything that is safe, your friends and family and security, is
behind that wall and you walk voluntarily into the unknown, into the maelstrom.
It's a great mental leap. You need to overcome all your fears."

Astonishingly, until Ousland's 1994 attempt to reach the North Pole solo and unsupported, he had never spent a night alone in a tent.

"In 1994, I went out of the helicopter. There was a gale force wind blowing in the
wrong direction. I saw 20 metres of open water in front of me. I skied to the east
along the ridge for two days and didn't know what to do or where to go. On the

Frozen food

third day the ice closed in and I managed to get across on thin ice. The first time you do it, it is so virgin and special. It will never be like that again. Nothing in life could give you that feeling again.

The first week it was horrible and I was afraid and I wanted to give up. Then I made some calculations. You don't have to be a psychologist to find solutions for a problem. The solutions are in you. I had to sum up the situation. I had food for two months, all my equipment was working and I was in good shape and I may as well keep going. I put my fears behind me and became more friends with the Arctic and pressure ridges, all those things which made me afraid and seemed to want me to go home. I got to the North Pole in 52 days.

It was a piece of cake!"

Death at Cape Artichesky

In 2004, ten years after Ousland's heroic expedition to the North Pole, five expeditions left Siberia with the same goal in mind. But that year a dark shadow was cast over Cape Artichesky. The conditions were so bad that three of the five expeditions arranged for a helicopter to fly them the 55 km over open water and onto the frozen arctic sea. The two remaining expeditions, both solo attempts by the French/Finnish Dominick Arduin and Frenchman, Frederic Chamard-Boudet left from Cape Artichesky. A full moon caused the tides to smash and crush the ice violently into the Cape's shoreline. Chamard-Boudet, hoping to be the first Frenchman to reach the Pole solo and unsupported, managed to ski 18 km around the lead before plunging into the icy water and losing his skis. He spent four minutes in the water but managed to haul himself onto his sledge and was rescued in a desperate state a day later by the Russians. He came within a whisper of losing his life.

Dominick Arduin, who had abandoned an attempt a year earlier due to frost bitten feet, was not so lucky. Two days after paddling out from Cape Artichesky she disappeared into the ice and was presumed drowned. Her body was never found. Not one of the expeditions in 2004 succeeded in their goal to reach the North Pole.

In 1995, buoyed up by his triumphant Arctic crossing, Ousland attempted a traverse at the other end of the globe. He reached a little beyond the South Pole when he was forced to abort the expedition with frostbite and blisters. The failed attempt rattled his confidence. It was one of the last classic challenges and sooner rather than later someone would do it. To be the first to cross Antarctica was what mattered to Ousland.

Early the following year he heard that his Polish friend Marek Kaminski, who had already walked to both North and South Poles in the same year, would attempt a solo traverse and then, irritatingly, word was out that Ranulph Fiennes was also setting out on the same challenge. Fiennes and Mike Stroud had crossed some 2000 kilometres of Antarctica unsupported in 1993. As often happens, a failed solo attempt such as Ousland's spurs on other adventurers, but Fiennes was especially hungry for this one. It was one of the few challenges left and if he succeeded it would be a huge public relations coup. It was also a chance to settle an old score with the Norwegian.

A group of six Koreans, led by Young Ho Heo, a two-fold conqueror of Everest, was also preparing for a traverse. Ousland's mind was made up, he would go again. The gauntlet thrown at the feet of each challenger specified that there would be no outside assistance in the way of food airdrops. Each man would haul his sledge carrying enough provisions to last him over some 3000 km in unimaginably harsh conditions.

With the help of a sports psychologist Ousland sifted through every atom of knowledge he had gained in past expeditions and worked on his strengths and weaknesses. Every detail of the expedition was scrutinised again and again. He was at his most meticulous best. His sledge, boots, skis and food were honed to perfection; he even cut his toothbrush in half and freeze-dried his food to save on weight. He believed that every gram he could save would make a difference both physically and mentally.

At the end of October the three competitors gathered in Punta Arenas where they were grounded by bad weather. Finally, it was safe enough for the six-hour flight to Patriot Hills in Antarctica.

Kaminski was of the same school as Ousland. His preparation was super-fastidious, to the extent that he saved 174 grams by transferring his films into condoms and discarding the original packaging. Both men had 'para-sails' to harness the wind. Fiennes's equipment, Ousland remarked, "was heavy and awkward and didn't seem to be well thought out." (*Alone across Antarctica* Borge Ousland)

Setting out from Berkner Island Ousland was faced with immense difficulties - bitter winds and whiteouts but also there were glorious days with fair winds that filled his sail and carried him south. His spirits soared. He crossed the ice shelf south of Berkner Island and with the aid of crampons hauled himself and his sledge through the Dufek Mountains, choosing an as yet unexplored route. Finally, one month in, he was on the plateau. News of his rivals was radioed to him.

Kaminski had met with an accident and had nearly been killed. Ensnared in his kite-lines and jerked off his feet, he hit his head on the icy surface. The semi-inflated kite dragged him unconscious across the icy terrain but in spite of concussion and serious leg injuries he continued.

Fiennes, meantime, was struggling up the hazardous Frost Spur glacier, a wall of crevassed ice, made even more terrifying by his not having packed his crampons. By the time Ousland was 500 kilometres ahead of his rivals, Fiennes had been forced to abandon his expedition in agony due to kidney stones.

Ousland admits to feeling genuinely sorry for Fiennes and also disappointed that he had dropped out. With Kaminski struggling to make any ground, the competition which had played a major role in motivating the Norwegian, was now gone. Fiennes sportingly sent a message asking Ousland to take particular care.

Ousland's account of the journey to the South Pole and beyond is nothing less than a litany of proof that man is not really made to withstand the extremes of the Antarctic continent. A combination of exhaustion, blistering cold and loneliness was taking its toll. Picking his way through crevasse fields, his ski pole would sometimes break through a snow bridge, revealing bottomless blue chambers below - a terrifying reminder of where he could end up. He faced kilometre upon kilometre of sastrugi - huge hillocks of frozen snow whipped up like thick double cream - that sapped every cell of energy from his body.

Yet there were also some days that he marvelled at the splendour of the Antarctic, embraced the silence and solitude and felt certain that he would arrive at a clearer understanding of himself and that which was important in life.

McMurdo Sound

McMurdo Station is an American scientific and logistics base which sits on the southern tip of Ross Island, approximately 3,500 km from New Zealand and supports up to 1,250 people. Besides its many buildings it boasts three airfields which service the American Amundsen/Scott South Pole base. Captain Scott's Discovery hut, built in 1901, stands near the harbour five km from the base. In 2003 McMurdo personnel held an anti-war protest against the invasion of Iraq by the USA. The base is overlooked by the awe-inspiring mountains, Mount Erebus, still actively volcanic, and Terror, the two sentinels often described by the early explorers.

In 1979 Air New Zealand Flight 901 crashed into Mt Erebus on a sightseeing flight killing, all 257 people on board. An incorrect computer-stored plan and bad visibility were to blame The Americans have constructed a 1,632 km 'road' called the McMurdo South Pole Highway from the base to the South Pole to service scientific vehicles. To construct the highway it was necessary to blow open crevasses with dynamite and refill them with snow to make the treacherous terrain passable. This, as it turns out, is a continuing process as crevasses continue to reappear due to the shifting ice shelves. It has raised serious environmental concerns about earth's most pristine environment. The US National Science Foundation claim the Highway will reduce air traffic to the South Pole as well as progress scientific exploration.

On the 19th December he reached the domed American Scientific Base at the South Pole. It was a five-hour bitter-sweet respite from his toils. Determined not to seek the comfort and warmth he so dearly craved, in case it broke the rhythm and routine of his journey, he refused even a mug of hot coffee. He collected some family letters to be opened on Christmas Eve, talked to his friend Sven Lidstrom, who was working at the base, and moved on.

Wracked by exhaustion and bouts of depression Ousland's steely determination didn't waver. Day after day, sometimes in -56°C, he pressed on, hauling and kiting, knowing he was on the 'downhill' run and heading towards the Axel Heiberg, a glacier that drops 3,000 metres in 15 kilometres. He dared not think of the fear that would grip him as he descended the icefall.

As Amundsen approached the glacier on his way to the South Pole in 1911, he wrote:

Here between the two mighty mountains it was just a mass of fissures within fissures, so huge and awful that one was tempted to believe that our progress in this direction was now barred.

It was a chilling descent that took 12 hours; one slip or slide by Ousland and both he and his sledge would have been sent 'to a cold and lonely grave.'

Finally Ousland was on the Ross Shelf with a thousand kilometres still to go. On his best day he sailed for 16 hours and covered 226 km. The Herculean effort, when he finally stopped, made him retch and wracked his body with cramp but by rigidly focusing on his goal, to be the first man to cross Antarctica solo, he rose above the physical agony.

Sixty-four days after leaving Berkner Island, Ousland skied into McMurdo Station. He had travelled 2,840 km across Antarctica and yet there were no banners to welcome him, just a mechanic working on an engine, who momentarily lifted his head, then carried on tinkering. 'You are the first person I have seen since the South Pole!' he announced.

Marek Kaminski and the Korean, Young Ho Heo had only just reached the South Pole; it was the end of their expeditions. The window for adventurers to remain in Antarctica had closed, and soon winter would be back. Ousland had achieved what others had failed to do since the time of Shackleton; he had crossed Antarctica under his own steam and he had done it alone. It would be 11 years before another adventurer, Rune Gjeldnes, would embark on a similar journey.

Ousland, cool, calculating and as tough as nails delivers the more esoteric side of his Polar wanderings in a clipped no nonsense manner.

"There is spirituality in nature. I look at eternal life after death as becoming the raindrop and falling back to the earth. I am talking about life after death but not like most Christians. I don't think I will meet my mother and father.
I think God is in nature. Eternal life after death is to become part of that raindrop that gives life to grass - to be part of the growth and thus part of God. I think there is a good side and a bad side and I try and stay on the good side.
These expeditions are coming away from human life. We are the rulers of the world but when you are out there you are tiny in the time frame."

He is clear that he does not believe in destiny but when opportunities present themselves a choice has to be made. Ousland says that in everyday life we see ourselves as important, even in the grand scheme of things, but on the ice fields one is humbled. You come to understand the dimension of being part of something much bigger than yourself. Once you realize that you have no part in the creation of the grandeur that surrounds you, you relinquish ego. He describes it as a state of Zen.

"Zen is like a state of meditation which is very physical. Through hardship you broaden your mind, the hardship is part of knowing yourself better. That is why people go into the mountains without food for 40 days. They want to get closer to Nirvana and the path to Nirvana is sacrifice.
Going on these expeditions means coming closer to that universe which is more or less away from human life."

He suggests that by 'peeling away' the layers of civilisation and trying to become part of the ice he builds a new world within the ice bound world, a letting go of the world as he knows it so that his tent becomes his home; his sledge, skis and ski-sticks extensions of his body. It is a method that allows him to endure months of solitude. 'This great whiteness and horror had to become my only reality.'

He is an iron-willed man and you believe him when he says he could be very rich if he wanted to but you equally understand it would be of no interest to him. His expeditions are what drive him and the lectures and books are a healthy by-product. Equally he has no truck with global warming issues although in 2001 he alerted people to the changes taking place in the North Pole.

> "You can't go to the North Pole for global warming. Don't go for the breast cancer society - its silly. What feels right to me is getting people into nature and making people love nature and so take their children out there. It is more important to get out there and to know what this great place is, rather than sit in a classroom reading scientific reports."

As an innovator Ousland has changed and influenced much of present day Polar travel. He redesigned the parasail in his attempt to snow kite across Antarctica in 1995 and then showed the world that with a few more tweaks to the sail it was possible to use it in the Arctic too. (Harnessing favourable winds is not a new way of travelling across Antarctica; both Scott and Shackleton attached sails to their sledges.)

Every piece of equipment he has worn, pulled and carried, or food he has prepared, he has re-shaped for optimum performance. A sledge that floats, skis to help lever you out of water, the ultimate polar boot, food recipes introducing extra fats and oils and perhaps the

Immersion suit and inventor – it works!

one piece of equipment that has taken Arctic adventurers into a new dimension, an immersion suit. Watching polar bears plunge into the water between flows inspired the 'dry' suit, a specially adapted overall which keeps you dry should you fall through thin ice or need to swim across leads of open water.

"Finding the right skis is so important, the boots, the bindings, these small details which can make you go five centimetres longer for each stroke. Being able to keep your skis on across the pressure ridges or able to move over the ice with as little resistance as possible. You have to work with nature."

On wearing the immersion suit for the first time in the Arctic.
The water was black and very deep, 4,000 metres to be exact, but despite that it was more than twenty degrees warmer than on land. Salt water freezes at -1°C and that was the usual water temperature in these parts. It would take a couple of hours before a thin crust of ice began to form on the lead. Small waves splashed against the ice bank; it didn't seem so daunting in good weather and I wasn't frightened, only very keyed up.
I wriggled into my suit and, holding the sledge rope in one hand, slid down into the water. The water pressed round my legs and I felt the adrenalin begin to surge. When I let go of the ice I floated gently out into the lead. Without the dry-suit, water would have spelt mortal danger, and my instincts were deeply ingrained. Small lumps of ice danced about my head in the ripples, but inside the thin skin it was dry and relatively pleasant. Gradually my fear of the water subsided and I breathed more calmly. How ludicrous it is, I thought. Here I am bobbing like an orange cork in a lead in the Arctic Ocean, and it's working! No one had done anything like it before me. Sometimes it's good to be a pioneer and this was definitely one of those occasions.

Alone across the North Pole Børge Ousland

Ousland has had innumerable encounters with polar bears but claims only one in a hundred might attack. During the North Pole traverse he described being transfixed with excitement when filming a mother with two half grown cubs as they came towards him. They were only five or six metres away before he fired the warning shot which headed them off.

Determined not to kill bears needlessly, he has had tiny steel pellets made for his 44 calibre magnum which when fired are painful but not fatal, However, if that doesn't work, the next slug in the chamber is a lead bullet. It was that which finished off the bear that attacked him and Erling Kagge as they neared the Pole during his 1990 expedition. When I asked him if he got it with one shot he reminded me he had been in the Special Forces!

"He wants to kill me because he is hungry, not because he doesn't like my face! You have to be alert at all times. A young male pops out from nowhere and comes

towards us. We shoot a warning shot and he doesn't react to that … he was aiming for us and we shot him. Bears charge on all fours. It was not painful for me to shoot him, I am a practical man."

To avoid the risk of the expedition being labelled 'supported' he and Kagge ignored the temptation to eat the meat there and then. Instead they sliced some pieces off the carcass and carried them to the North Pole. Not only were they coming to the end of their provisions but also they had been living off the same food every day for two months, and they consumed the meat with relish. Ironically, as already mentioned before, their expedition today is considered supported, due to one of their team members being airlifted off the ice.

It should be noted that Polar bear liver is dangerously toxic due to high levels of Vitamin A and should be avoided.

In 2001 Ousland set out to be the first person to ski and parasail across the Arctic Ocean solo and without resupplies. It was a decision of extraordinary courage. Two compatriots, Rune Gjeldnes and Torry Larsen had crossed the ocean a year earlier without re-supplies and it had nearly cost them their lives.

The start from Cape Artichesky could not have been shakier. He was surrounded by ice, too saline to melt for drinking and cooking water. Exhausted and thirsty he took to his tent only to be woken up by the deafening sound of an angry sea crushing and splintering the floes around him but by pure chance the piece of ice he was camping on was left intact. The following day the sea calmed and he managed to scrape crystals off the ice to drink. Just as things were improving on the ice his sledge broke.

He agonised as to whether he should give up. If a new sledge was brought in his status of 'unsupported' would not hold but worse than that he questioned whether he still had the motivation to continue. The full horror of his mortality was as crystal sharp as the ice that surrounded him.

He then considered doing what many adventurers I have interviewed have admitted to - fabricating a physical injury, as an excuse to give up. He felt ashamed of himself.

Calls on his iridium satellite telephone to the people he relied on most in his life and much soul searching gave him the courage he was looking for. He arranged for a new sledge to be flown in. He would dump half the food and carry much less weight on the new sledge and arrange for a re-supply at the North Pole.

Eighty-two days later Ousland arrived at Ward Hunt Island in Canada. He'd had a new sledge brought in at the beginning of the expedition and he had been given a re-supply of food at the North Pole but yet again he had stepped into the record books as the first person to ski alone across both Poles and, better than that, he had beaten his demons.

In 2006 Ousland was to return to Cape Artichesky when he teamed up with the South African adventurer Mike Horn to walk and ski to the North Pole unsupported, in the darkness of the Arctic winter. Besides the audacity of the expedition, these two men were cut from very different cloth - the tall, quiet blonde Norwegian, known for his 'picky' attention to detail and the dark, thick set, gregarious South African, a chancer, a maverick who flies by the seat of his pants.

When courage ebbs away and everything seems hopeless, there is only one thing to do: open your eyes to a new path to your goal. Let go of what has been, take a step sideways and find a new road. If need be, take a step back to enable you to take two forwards later.   It really isn't that different from human evolution itself. Everything that doesn't work is expunged by selection and new directions materialise. At times, almost total annihilation is needed so that the best can live on and become even better.

Alone Across the North Pole Borge Ousland

Both had succeeded in their own solo challenges and now this odd couple were embarking on the toughest challenge of their lives.

For the layman it is hard to understand the apocalyptic icescape of the Arctic, a jumble of broken ice ramparts that mount each other in grotesque forms and ridges many metres high and barring the way forward. They sap every bit of energy, both physically and mentally as you drag your sledge over them. Kilometres achieved on one day can be obliterated by 'negative drift' the next as the currents beneath the ice inexorably sweep you away from your goal.

Constant scanning of the landscape is necessary, searching for safe ice, detouring around leads, picking the best way through pressure ridges and watching for polar bears. In daylight it is possible to make some sense of this landscape gripped in an icy turmoil but what if all you can see is caught in the single beam of light thrown from a torch, banded around your head?

"It is so intense because you are walking inside a tunnel. Everything else is black and you can see only ten to fifteen metres in front of you; the rest you can't see. You have to use your senses in a different way. Then, after some weeks the full moon comes out and there is this ghost-like landscape. It's bleak, like another ice planet.

Your senses get over loaded, that is why we got so tired; we wanted to sleep all the time. Light gives energy and there was no light.

Everything flashes by in a blizzard and there are two men out there 1000 km from the nearest people: two people with their headlights just seeing the ground in front of them. It's a great feeling, a thrill. Mike and I were in a constant war zone, in no-man's land. We became like brothers.

Mike has bad circulation in his fingers. He doesn't get enough blood to his fingers but his feet were perfect. My feet were just so cold."

Three weeks away from the Pole, Horn began to flounder: it was soon obvious to Ousland that his team-mate was dangerously ill. They both knew it was some sort of an infection, possibly from frostbite, but Horn refused to buckle and, to make matters worse, he also refused to take medicine. Ousland knew that sheer will alone was keeping Horn going. He

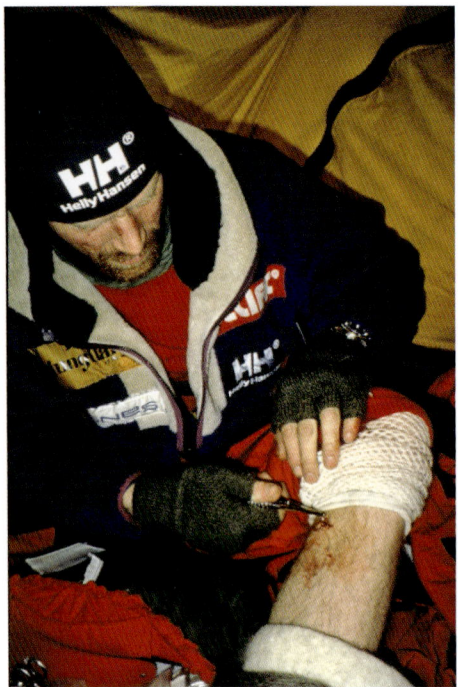

Running repairs

had never witnessed anything like it before. Horn was literally bleeding from every orifice.

"Mike had an infection from frostbite in his fingers, he had blood poisoning. If he hadn't had antibiotics I think he would have died. If he pressed his thumb pus would come out and that was three weeks before we reached the North Pole. He didn't want to take medicine.
I gave him a double dose of antibiotics. He has such strong will power. He was bleeding from his nose and his arse, it infected his whole system."

On the sixtieth day, as the Arctic was swathed in a pastel hue of the dawning of the first summer sun, Horn and Ousland reached the Pole. They had ski-ed, hauled, swum and grappled their way north. It was now just a matter of waiting for the helicopter to take them back to safety and rush Horn to urgent medical care.

They referred to themselves as brothers and both agreed they had learnt from the other. Ousland's attention to detail, 'my strict German routine' and Horn's tendency to find solutions along the way, did not always produce a perfect combination. Horn's insistence on using his cooking pot as both something to cook and crap in, a plastic bag used as a liner for the latter, was not Ousland's way of doing things. Horn then agreed to perform his daily function in the vestibule of the tent. The two highly motivated and competitive men met half way to find a solution.

It is unlikely the expedition will ever be repeated. It took two of the fittest, bravest and above all experienced adventurers to reach the North Pole during the Arctic winter and it took them to a fine line, not only between success and failure but life and death.

'The important thing is not how I die but how I have lived' is Ousland's maxim but the will to live when the chips are down is what counts.

Web site:	www.borgeousland.com
Books:	In the Footsteps of Nansen
	Alone Across Antarctica
	Alone to the North Pole

POLAR GUIDES

Too often in the flag waving, goal reaching moment clients forget who got them there. Frequently the guides name is omitted when the expedition is recounted for sponsors, friends or the media. It's a hazard that goes with the job.

Often it is lack of ego that separates the guide from the adventurer.

Guiding clients safely is the objective, rather than reaching the destination, which cannot be guaranteed. A fat fee does not mean certain success. For now, with only a handful of Polar guides and limited expeditions trying to reach the Poles the balance between safety, success and financial pressures is held in check. It is a fine balance but commercialisation is waiting in the wings. Some quarters believe it will be only a matter of time before hard currency and the need to deliver overrides caution and blurs the boundaries. It has happened on Everest. Unthinkable only a few years ago, men have perished on the mountain while both guides and climbers have looked the other way in their determination to reach the summit.

Icebergs towering like cathedrals

GEOFF SOMERS MBE

*"When guiding, your mind races with statistics.
You are constantly checking your watch. You become
a time freak. It's the most expensive way of being
miserable. It's all navigation and logistics."*

Geoff Somers, in his late 50s, is a wiry, tough man with pale blue, deep set eyes and in spite of a shock of thinning grey hair, looks much younger than his age. He is as fit as a racing greyhound with the physique typical of a fell runner, a sport he practises in his beloved Lake District in the north west of England.

He lives in a distinctly bachelor house, practical, devoid of the feminine touch and decorated with all-weather gear. It was surprising not to find his trusty bicycle propped up in the kitchen.

The son of a doctor with Victorian principles, his childhood was spent playing with his three siblings and avoiding other children. Crushingly shy throughout his young adult life he recalls the agony of merely having to speak to people and the embarrassment he felt when he mustered up the courage to join in a conversation at college, only to have one of his peers announce in mock amazement to the gathering, 'He speaks!'

Today, a little less shy, he describes himself as a control freak, a nanny, a bully, cold, calculating and dictatorial. Yet he is venerated by the clients he has guided. Rosie Stancer, trained by Somers for her North Pole solo attempt, describes him as her guru, while Katherine Hartley dedicated her book *To the Poles Without a Beard* to him.

*"I am very strict, dictatorial and I drive people up the wall. I get angry inside.
Some people are much better at putting their personalities across and getting
people to do things. Paul Landry is also very strict but he has a much easier
personality. He is straight down the line. It's like controlling the sledge dogs, you
can be affectionate in one way but they have to know exactly where they stand."*

After qualifying as a carpenter and joiner he worked in an Outward Bound organisation until the age of 21. By chance he was shown slides of the Antarctic and he knew that was where he needed to go. He applied for a job as guide for the British Antarctic Survey (BAS) who were looking for someone who was tough, used to communal living and had carpentry skills to help build a new wing at the Antarctic base. It was as if Somers was made to order. The isolation of the vast white continent suited the shy young man although he still found it difficult to sit around the bar of an evening and converse with BAS staff. But once out in the white wilderness running his team of nine huskies he was utterly at home.

"The dogs were incredibly useful. We travelled right through the winter and you really learnt about your environment. Nowadays, all the Antarctic authorities are paranoid about accidents because people don't have the experience. With dogs you learn about walking on sea ice, you feel it, you learn about the weather. In a vehicle you feel vulnerable, yet on snowmobiles you can do 100 km a day and when you have a static camp your snow mobile doesn't eat any fuel."

Somers' fondness for the huskies did not tip into sentimentality any more than it did in the Edwardian age when the explorer's food source depended on eating the dogs.

"They are working dogs, I have shot many a dog while working in Antarctica. If you were hungry of course you would eat them. These are not pets, they are not your mates and I certainly wouldn't bring them home to meet my mum!"

The Husky Ban
In 1991 the nations of the Antarctic Treaty System agreed on a Protocol to protect Antarctica. In 1994 the ban of huskies came into force after fears the dogs could transmit diseases such as canine distemper to the seal population, a theory which is challenged. Today motorised sledges (skidoos) are used at the scientific bases but many scientists and adventurers feel the loss of the dogs deeply. They have played a crucial role in the survival of men since the turn of last century. Reliable and strong, a team of nine dogs can pull a sledge load of 450 kilos all day but, above all, the companionship they provided is irreplaceable.

In the mid '80s the American explorer, Will Steger, was looking for a Briton to join his multinational trans-Antarctic expedition which included Victor Boyarsky and Jean Louis Etienne, the first person to walk solo to the North Pole. Antarctica had only ever been crossed with motorised vehicles, by Vivien Fuchs and Edmund Hilary, in 1958, and later by Ran Fiennes using snowmobiles. 'I thought it was all a bit stupid but I was willing to give it a go,' said Somers. It was an epic journey, that first dog sledge traverse of Antarctica. It took three years to plan and 374 days to complete. Later Somers trained the 20 women for the 1997 McVities Relay Polar Challenge where he first met Rosie Stancer and Ann Daniels.

"Ann Daniels arrived totally ignorant as to what a snow flake was like and she has turned out a natural for Polar travel, very tough but still feminine like the Amazonian women. Well they were supposed to be beauties weren't they?"

Rosie Stancer?

"Scatterbrained!"

Obviously very fond of her, he continued to train her as she completed two more expeditions, both to the South Pole. The first, a self guided five-woman team, was followed by a solo unsupported expedition, when she was only just beaten by the British woman Fiona Thornewill.

> *"She wouldn't put on weight, she couldn't read a map or compass or light the stove. She learnt how to put up a tent because you have to learn to do these things on your own. She would ring me on her mobile when she was training. "Geoff, I am up in Scotland, I can't get my stove to work!" I didn't want her to do the trip at all. She set out 12 hrs after Fiona Thornewill. I saw her off. She arrived at the Pole a day after Fiona, having done 30 more miles as she had left something behind so she had to backtrack but she did the trip faster."*

More recently Somers was guide during the making of the BBC television documentary 'Blizzard - Race to the Poles' with the British ex-commando and television star, Bruce Parry. The documentary, filmed in Greenland, was a re-enactment of the 1910 'race' between Scott and Amundsen to the South Pole. As in the 1910 expedition, the Norwegians far out played and outran the British. Somers conceded that the British team, led by Parry, was not only pitched against some of the greatest Norwegian Polar experts of today, including Rune Gjeldnes, but they were hampered by a lack of time to train with their unruly huskies. If that wasn't enough, they became ill through eating pemmican (concentrated mixture of fat and protein) made from pig lard. But his sympathy stopped there.

"The Norwegians had a routine which the Brits didn't. The British team would lie in and make excuses if the alarm didn't go off. Erling Kagge, the first person to reach the South Pole solo and unsupported in 1991, advised only one thing: 'get up in the morning!' You get up and you have to start and you have to walk for eight hours. It's no use sitting down and looking at the view.

You need your dogs for months to train them. On this trip they had a couple of weeks and you can't run a team of dogs like that. They didn't have time for training as it rained the three weeks we spent in the village before going on the ice cap and you couldn't train the dogs in the slush. The Brits had the worst dogs and they had no lead dog and the Norwegians were incredibly experienced, having one of the top dog mushers in the world.

The other thing which was a disaster was the pemmican. It was made in the UK with beef fat but the Greenlanders said they couldn't bring it in so they made one with pork fat which is not the same, it's revolting. It looked like a bowl of fat when they melted it! When I worked in BAS guys who had been away on dog sledges for three months would just crave butter. If you start out on a trip you cannot go onto summit rations straight away, your body just rejects it. These lads in Greenland had to start on 75% pork fat which is horrible."

I had first heard of Somers when reading Katherine Hartley's book *To the Poles Without a Beard.* It was a self deprecating account of a London wild child turned good as she faced the challenges of sledge hauling to the South Pole with a team of amateurs, guided by Somers.

"I was intensely worried about Katherine Hartley from the moment I saw her. She plays on being 'ditsy.' On day one I thought what am I in this for? She drove me nuts and needed total care. She got frost nip on the first day. But she did the whole trip and she never complained and when we finished I thought she was number one, the best in the group. There were other people who were super macho. I was hoping they would be the best but they are the ones I would leave behind."

Katherine Hartley's regime of minimal training and a diet of cigarettes and booze is not recommended and her suffering and lack of confidence particularly at the start of her expedition is well recorded in her book but Somers believes it is all about a mental state.

"I know of people who have done no training. Some people who go on guided trips are fit, pulling tyres running and mountaineering but are a wash-out when it comes to hauling sleds for 60 days; they are useless because it's all in the head. I am a nanny and a bully but I have never had anybody fail or drop out although the closest I got was Katherine Hartley. I have taken over 60 people to the North Pole, some just the last degrees and I don't want anyone to fail. It's just not an option."

Whilst working for BAS he joined the 'Antarctic swimming club' when he fell through the sea ice and found himself treading water. On another occasion, a person attached to him by a rope disappeared into a crevasse. Did he turn to God at these moments?

"Absolutely not! God disappeared out of the window when I left school. I was going to go into the priesthood but the priests and bishops were all squabbling and I wondered why God couldn't make up his mind! I have been in some very frightening situations and got away with them but my greatest fear was at public school. We had a marks period once every two weeks and if you didn't do well it was read out at assembly and followed by a beating. I would squirm with fear of the beatings. I was afraid of the physical pain."

Somers has been gonged with an MBE and Polar Medal for the Trans- Antarctic expedition. He did not appear remotely interested in either.

"I am flattered but not proud. People who knew me pushed for the MBE rather than the people who should have pushed for it like the Royal Geographic Society or science institutions. Anyway, I did it for myself not the community."

Today's most respected guide says his guiding days are over unless someone makes him an offer he cannot refuse. He has guided for 20 years covering 10,000 miles on the polar plateaux. The huge physical and mental effort has taken its toll.

"You get two months pay, you spend seven months preparing and the rest of the time recovering. So much of the year is involved in organising the trips. I don't have the energy to do anything else. It's only in the last couple of years I have reached a tax bracket. I won't miss it."

Somers agrees he is accused of underplaying his achievements.

"It's a modern thing to stand on a pedestal. It's nice just to be part of the Keswick community playing tennis and my flute and dancing!"

MATTY MCNAIR

"If you are losing more weight than planned, you are on an expedition, if you are gaining more weight than planned, you are on a vacation!"

Size doesn't seem to matter. The American Matty McNair, one of the most experienced Polar guides today, is diminutive. She reminded me of a weather-beaten Mona Lisa but behind the gentle eyes and enigmatic smile is a no-nonsense woman.

We met in the clamour of a west London café on one of her trips to England where she was organising the 2008 Race to the South Pole.

She was born in Pennsylvania and, at the age of two weeks, took her first trip in a canoe, which set the pattern for the rest of her life. She has climbed, kayaked, dog sledged, hiked, kited and skied up down and around just about everything.

Like Landry and Somers she worked for the Outward Bound schools before moving to Iqaluit, (which means 'many fish'), Canada's smallest capital situated on Baffin Bay where she brought up her two children with her now ex husband Paul Landry. Iqaluit, formerly Frobisher Bay, has a population of around 6,000, the majority of whom are Inuit. It can only be accessed by air, snowmobile, boat or dog sledge. It is a harsh, treeless environment that suits McNair and her teams of huskies and her house is often used as a watering hole for those adventurers preparing for Arctic challenges. McNair holds her own Polar records including leading an unsupported 52 day expedition to the South Pole only to turn around and kite back to the start with her children in an astonishing 17 days.

"I like to give people the physical and emotional skills to achieve things they think they can't. It doesn't bother me that I don't get into the limelight when guiding. What bothers me is when someone claims to have led the expedition and they haven't even looked at the map. There is a history of making false claims, it's all ego, driven by having to raise funds. I had a client who kept on jumping up and down saying I am going to be the youngest person to the Pole and I said oh yeah, I am going to be the first to have the menopause!"

Talking of which I wondered, having guided a gaggle of women relaying to the North Pole with another female guide, Denise Martin, what are the differences between her male and female clients?

"Women have a little more trouble with letting go of things; women want to talk

about everything and analyse it. They can't do much of that during the day but they can in the tent. The guys just want to get on with it, they are ready to let go and move on, it doesn't have to be talked about. When you come to a difficult spot women will automatically help each other whereas, the men just watch other men heaving over the pressure ridges."

McNair has a reputation for bringing her clients through the rigours of Polar travel fairly unscathed and she has some hard and fast rules. While guiding the same women's relay team to the North Pole the women listened in to the radio reports of a Dutch team on the ice at the same time and two very different stories were unfolding.

"The Dutch were suffering with frostbite, saying how hard it all was but we were having a blast. In the tent we would strip down and take sponge baths, just enjoying ourselves. There is a small margin for error. It's important to put out only 80 per cent of your energy, don't use 100 per cent. Once you reach burnout you can't bounce back. For instance, if you go through the ice you will die if you are too tired to recover yourself. You can avoid the cold, eat before you are hungry, drink before you are dehydrated, stop before you are exhausted, take off your Parka before you sweat and put it on before you get cold. I think if someone freezes their fingers they have made some critical errors - it shouldn't happen."

McNair admits that early on into an expedition she has to establish that she is 'boss dog' as often she is working with people who, in their normal lives, have top positions. She says she 'kicks butt' just as easily as she nurtures her clients.

"People need to be primed mentally and physically, their expectations need to be formed before we get on the ice."

She reflected on one of the few times she felt truly afraid when guiding. During the Tom Avery expedition, a re-enactment of Robert Peary's 1909 North Pole expedition,

Girls best friend

she was skiing ahead of the four men and dog teams. Without warning, a ground storm blew up shrouding the landscape in a whiteout.

> " I looked back and I couldn't see the dogs and my tracks were blown over. I thought to myself, I don't have anything with me; no 'phone or radio and it's hard to imagine how huge it is out there. In minutes you can lose people and never find them. I had lost two teams and four guys! If you stare at the snow long enough you can see the faint shadows of where the skis have been. I marked them with a pile of snow as a cairn and eventually I found them. I am not sure if the boys even missed me!"

The question of belief covers a broad spectrum. Each adventurer has their own interpretation of God and spiritual experiences, highlighted by the extremes of nature, physical pain or the threat of danger.

> "I feel that there are forces, energy fields. I had a very hard day one day going to the South Pole, I knew Paul was with his lover. My feet were in excruciating pain and it was difficult to keep up. There were ice crystals in the air and I felt something drifting, floating beside me, off to my left. It was the spirit of my grandmother. She was in lavender and bare foot and she was waving and smiling. My grandmother was a doctor, she travelled and taught at the university of Cairo and she was my spiritual mentor. I like to be open to the possibility of guardian angels."

The dark winter months of 1916 had seemed one unending blizzard. During the lulls, Wild and Gaze joined Joyce in training the puppies. The progeny of Nell and Bitchie were nearly ready to pull in a team, they were the lucky survivors. Seven pups had died in accidents, and the overstressed Nell had attacked and eaten several. Sickened by the relentless savagery, Gaze shot her. Joyce skinned any suitable carcasses to make mittens, reserving his sentiment for Oscar, Gunner, Towser, and Conrad.

The Lost Men - The Harrowing Story of Shackleton's Ross Sea Party.
Kelly Tyler- Lewis Published by Bloomsbury

I asked Rosie Stancer, who was guided by McNair on the all-women's North Pole relay, to describe her. 'To be in the company of Matty', she said, 'was like being in an electrical storm with sparks of energy flying in all directions but she didn't waste time on idle chatter. She and Denise (Martin) were the real heroines, shepherding 20 hopelessly amateur women over the treacherous ice to the North Pole.' On one occasion, as the women hauled and heaved their pulks in stoic silence, Stancer glanced back to see McNair doubled over in what she thought was extreme distress. She unhitched her pulk and ran back to find McNair, nose to the ground marvelling at the shape of ice crystals. That, she says, sums her up.

"Peter Pan is one of my mentors because when you think happy thoughts you can fly. With negative thoughts, dragging your pulk feels like dragging a dead horse, your legs start to hurt and you think the runners are iced up. You survive by breaking things up into small parts, into a day, into hours, into one step at a time, otherwise it's all so overwhelming."

It is true is that with all the Polar bear encounters, and most people I have spoken to have had them, there have been no reports of injuries, let alone fatalities, although everyone appears to have had a close call at some time or other. Statistics show that in the past 30 years, seven people have been fatally wounded by polar bears, one in Alaska over the same period and 19 in Russia since records began.

McNair on the great Peary debate

In 2005 the young British adventurer, Tom Avery, with three other men, Andrew Gerber, George Wells and Hugh Dale-Harris, with McNair as their guide, set out with dog teams to prove that it was possible to reach the North Pole in 37 days as claimed by Peary in 1909. They reached the North Pole in 37 days with hours to spare. Their expedition may not attract quite as much dissension as Peary's, but it is dismissed out of hand by the sceptics on the grounds that the argument is not whether Peary reached the Pole in 37 days but the distance he claims to have covered in a day. "Avery didn't do the speed Peary did even for a day. He was fitter, stronger and better equipped. He should have done it twice as fast," says the Canadian, Richard Weber an expert on the Arctic. McNair stands firm.

"If he (Peary) wanted to fake it he would have done it before. He tried numerous times and got very close. People say that Peary wasn't taking sightings everyday, but you don't need to, you have the sun. We estimated with dead reckoning - guessing our distance over a two-week period and we were 10 nautical miles short when we had estimated how far we had done. It takes skill to drive dogs; Peary had the best teams in the world, Greenlanders, driven by Greenlanders. People ask why Peary didn't write in his journal that he had reached the Pole. He did it later. (This raised suspicion as to whether he had reached the North Pole at all.) Well, I didn't write anything when I reached the Pole either. I was exhausted, words don't come to mind. I was tired and hungry and cold and I needed to tie the dogs up. Unless you have experienced it you don't get it." Richard Weber disagrees vehemently. Both he and Mikhail Malakhov could only cover 4km an hour on their final ski dash to the Pole in 1995, in spite of carrying nothing more than light backpacks. It is impossible that Peary could have covered up to twice that distance an hour, having lost most of his toes to frostbite, he says.

All the same, simply coming across their spoor on the ice is enough to set the adrenalin pumping. Borge Ousland, cool as ever, made the snap decision that the bear charging him meant business, so he shot it. Somehow, you can't help thinking pint size women like Rosie

Stancer and McNair out on the ice would make a handy snack for the world's largest carnivore which can stand eight feet tall and weigh anything up to 600 kilograms.

"I have a lot of respect for polar bears because they are unpredictable. Hungry bears are dangerous bears and I have had a polar bear come right up to the line of tents. I threw a flare at one once and it sniffed it and ate it. When I travel with dogs they will warn me of bears. The dogs are very aggressive towards them and will chase them out of camp."

Iqaluit's temperature does not rise above freezing for eight months of the year and the majority of people are Inuit. Their chosen form of transport may be snowmobiles today but McNair is enraptured by her Canadian Inuit sledge dogs. She can run a team of 22 dogs, each tied by separate lines to the sledge in a formation called "fan hitch," her whip and voice steering them over the snow. Until the introduction of snowmobiles, survival depended on the dogs and the Inuit took no prisoners. The dogs were expected to pull up to two weeks on empty stomachs. Any aggression shown and they were swiftly dispatched and turned into fur mittens and pants.

"When I say down they say 'Yes M'am!' When I stop they need to go down so as not to get tangled. If they bolt off I could lose my life out there. It's important they don't fight when they are in harness and I never play with them if they are in harness. My top dog will break up a fight and he reprimands anyone who starts it. I use body language and stare at them aggressively. It's down or I am going to thump you, and you have to mean what you say. They test me all the time."

Every team has a lead dog, obviously the one hitched at the front of the team. Surprisingly, it's not always the boss dog.

"A boss dog is the king, he gets first rights at females and is not necessarily the lead dog. A boss dog may not like to lead because he can't see what is going on behind him. The lead dog is usually in the middle of the hierarchy, no threat to anybody and everybody likes it. I have dogs that know the calls but the other dogs won't follow them; like some humans they don't have leadership ability!"

Time and again, without any prompting, the adventurers I interviewed returned to the subject of coming to terms with everyday life after an expedition. Bewildered, it takes time to rise to the surface of reality and to normal life again. It is a step-by-step process, like a deep-sea diver avoiding the bends. There is a sense of loss after an expedition, a feeling of detachment and sometimes more seriously, depression.

"When you have been on these expeditions, your life is reduced to a tent, a pulk and a goal and you are so focused. For me after the North Pole, I was just drifting, my kids had become teenagers, my family coped without me and I had no purpose or direction. I call it Polar shock. I still saw whiteness all around me and

the wind was blowing through my mind. It's a spiritual high and trying to come back to earth again is very difficult. You can't share it with people because they don't understand the loneliness and emptiness inside. I understand why people like Shackleton wanted to go back and touch something they had."

I suggested living in Iqaluit, cold and dark for much of the year was a lonely life for a woman on her own but she simply gave that enigmatic smile.

"I can hook up my dogs and head out. I can head out for weeks and not see anyone. It's endless. That's a real sense of spirituality."

Web site: www.northwinds.arctic.com
Books: On Thin Ice - A Woman's Journey to the North Pole

PAUL LANDRY

"On reaching the Pole I am only the photographer!"

Interestingly, the French Canadian guide Paul Landry and the Briton, Geoff Somers, share many characteristics and none more so than their innate shyness.

Landry spent 15 years living in Iqaluit, on Baffin Island in the Canadian Arctic with his now ex-wife, the guide Matty McNair. Together they ran their teams of dogs and guided numerous expeditions to the Poles. Their two children, Sarah and Eric, both in their early 20s and having grown up in an Arctic playground have already achieved exceptional Polar records. They are undoubtedly the future stars of Polar adventure.

I first met Landry, who describes himself as having a passion for politics, scotch, coffee, kiting and music, in the city of Montreal, where he now lives with his girlfriend.

The first impression was of a quiet, intense man, not too tall but extremely athletic, his face lined from years of squinting into the harsh Polar sun. He is tough yet emotional, which was demonstrated when I asked him at our first meeting about the medal he had received from the Canadian government for rescuing a drowning man from the torrents of an icy river. He was surprised I knew about it and to date had only ever spoken about the dramatic episode to his family. Recounting how he and a friend came close to losing their own lives during the rescue, he wept. The more I got to know Landry, the more I realised it was typical of him to remain silent where others might not.

Like Somers, he cut his teeth working for the Outward Bound schools. Although familiar with the Arctic he was 47 years old before he guided his first trip to the Magnetic North Pole. He has reached the North Pole four times, twice with dog sledges, the South Pole four times followed by the Pole of Inaccessibility.

"You have to put in your time and pay your dues. Guide people on small outings and at the same time push yourself in these environments. But if I want to get to the Poles and break records, I do that on my personal trips. You have to differentiate between experience and skills. You can take a course of crevasse rescue which is great. If you fall into a crevasse you can get yourself out but that doesn't mean you know how to detect a crevasse. Look at Scott and Shackleton, they prepared for their expeditions but didn't get experience, whereas the Norwegians, they invested lots of time on the glaciers and in the Canadian arctic. I want to be clear that not everyone needs to be guided but they need to go out and get experience.

The Polar community has really changed a lot in the last few years. The emphasis seems to be on breaking records and making claims. People went down because they had a dream. Today people are looking at going because they want to be recognised and they have zero interest in that environment."

While writing this book one of the most difficult things has been to gauge how difficult it really is to tackle the Poles. What some have made sound easy, others have described as feats of horrific hardship and danger. Landry casts some light on the subject.

"Richard Weber has devoted his life to the Arctic Ocean and has got serious experience. He views it differently to say Ran Fiennes or your new adventurer. He has a guiding company and he wants clients, so he is going to present information which is inviting because he wants people to sign up. He is going to talk about the chances of success and minimize risk.
Ran Fiennes earns his living writing books and lecturing. The public is interested in drama and he delivers. Then you have the young and inspiring adventurer who wants a company to sponsor him. What model is he going to use? Weber's where it's all do-able and safe or Ran's that has the perfect media hook? You can replace these names with lots of others. Antarctica is a holiday; I believe that. It's great down there but when you compare that to Ran's book it is the harshest place on earth."

I wondered where Landry fitted into all of this?

"Do I have to be in that? I am a song and dance man like Bob Dylan and I play

my music. I would put myself next to Richard but I don't have as much experience as he does on the Arctic Ocean but I have more guiding experience than him. I will tell you a story. I took two clients down to the South Pole, one was a young Finnish PE teacher, probably born with skis on his feet. The other client was English, had hardly been on snow before and was 22 kilos overweight. Both very nice individuals. If you read each of their books, you would be convinced they had been on separate trips. The Finn was at home and the British man was overwhelmed with the environment and his physical capabilities. They both had two completely different experiences."

Landry on the great Peary debate.

Shackleton left Elephant Island in the James Caird boat. Suicidal attempt. Shackleton's chance of success? Nil. Had they perished and there was no evidence found, the public today would say he never made it, there was no hope in hell he could make it. He did something that was extraordinary and that is very difficult to understand. Peary did the same thing at a certain time in history that is very difficult for us to understand today. For that he has been criticised. Reinhold Messner climbed Everest solo in three days; the mountaineering community said it's impossible! Some things may never be repeated. Certain elements come together at the right time. If Weber and Malakhov tried to reach the North Pole and back again, they may not make it. It was phenomenal and it may not be repeated. Peary by profession was a surveyor and he was a brilliant navigator. Matthew Henson was also a brilliant navigator and then you have the Inuit. I travelled extensively with the Inuit hunters and there are things I have experienced which I cannot explain. They have a sense of their world. Peary had the best Arctic traveller that ever lived, the Inuit, Oohtah, like Shackleton who had the best navigator, Frank Worsley. Oohtah is a folk hero within Inuit history. He had Ooqueah, Egingwah and Seegloo who were brilliant. They would go out off the coast of Greenland to hunt and they were on rough ice, moving ice. They didn't have compasses and they came back. They knew how to navigate and it's a different method of navigation. I don't know if Peary made it to the exact North Pole but I believe he came within the vicinity; to me it doesn't matter. Peary did not take longitude readings but he understood 'drift.' He nearly died in 1906 when he ended up in Greenland instead of Ellesmere because of drift. Peary has been challenged for his speeds but he had the best dog drivers that ever walked the face of this earth. It's the biggest Polar controversy and it will never be proven.

Landry doesn't come cheap. If you want to hire him he charges something in the region of 600 American dollars a day plus all his expenses. The client must supply all equipment, kites, pulks etc. and Landry has the option of keeping them after the expedition.

"I let my clients decide what they want to do and then I will say whether I come on board or not. People pay me for when things go wrong."

I have used ExplorersWeb, the website run by the adventurers Tina and Tom Sjogren, countless times while researching *Ice Tracks*. The information on their website has been invaluable and many of their stories are not only informative but inspirational. Yet, they have come under fire from many in the Polar community, including Landry, a personal friend of theirs, in particular on the prickly subject of the first time adventurer John Wilton-Davies who attempted a solo march to the South Pole.

> *"If you fall into a crevasse and you are roped up to someone they can pull you out but when you are solo it is a different story. ExplorersWeb ran a five part series on John Wilton-Davies and how he prepared for his expedition. Thousands of people a day read that website and the message is that it is okay to go out like that. As a professional it's not okay. It's great that people take on all these challenges and they don't have to hire a guide, but if they don't, they should get some experience, otherwise it's reckless. Someone or many in the future will die. ExplorersWeb is very biased and it is seen that way by the professionals. It defines expeditions to be supported and unsupported. It was incredibly disrespectful to Rune Gjeldnes during his Antarctic crossing in saying his kite was a form of support. Using a kite is the same as using a flotation device. It aids you and you are not receiving outside assistance."*

Often the greatest challenges to expeditions is the cohesiveness of the group, and never more so than on Polar expeditions. The isolation of the daily marches, the constant anxiety about keeping up with the group and the confined tent living at the end of the day are the dramas played out. Group dynamics invariably change after the first week when the euphoria of the expedition starts to wane and people care more about their own ability to succeed than someone else's well being.

> *"I try to set a tone that it is okay to make mistakes and laugh about it and tease each other. You need to be committed to the Pole but at the same time not take yourselves too seriously. I had a client with haemorrhoids and that's not unusual. He was way back and I said to one of the other clients, what the hell is happening to so and so and he said he has haemorrhoids. I said, why the hell are we travelling then; let's set up the tent and I will call the doctor at Patriot Hills and yes, he will be the laughing stock of the staff there! Chaffing is a big thing, under the armpits and between the cheeks of your bum and your thighs.*
> *I am very ambitious and driven but it can be stressful and I have to remind myself to lighten up but ultimately I am responsible for safety. On the Arctic Ocean there are days when the ice pack is moving and I have to make many decisions. I don't think anyone could die but someone could fall into the water or the team could become separated and this wears you down.*
> *If I feel scared I do something about it. I try to teach people to assume more responsibility. I want people to finish the expedition and to feel they have done it on their own. I don't want people to say they wouldn't have done it without me."*

"As we reach the height of the Somoveken glacier the view ahead reminds me of Canada, more specifically, the prairie provinces in winter. Flat or slightly undulating snowfields greet the eye in all directions. To think it will be similar for the next 2,000 km is awesome. Some would call it boring. But to the accustomed eye, there are always subtle changes in the snow texture, the light, the big sky or the cloud patterns. To appreciate such beauty one must open one's mind and emotions to this place. One must tread lightly but with comfort and style to enjoy this pristine beauty. Antarctica does not share itself with those who come to conquer her in order to boost their egos."

Paul Landry guiding the expedition to the Pole of Inaccessibility in 2006/2007

Kiting is changing the face of Polar travel, particularly in Greenland and Antarctica and we are seeing a shift from the traditional methods of skiing and man hauling sleds. Harnessing the wind by attaching sails to sleds has been used since the turn of the 1900s. Today the kites are attached to waist harnesses and the traveller is sandwiched between pulk and kite. Kites vary from 3 metres to 12 metres, depending on the strength of the wind and the weight of the pulk. Ten times the distance can be covered in a day compared to the trudge of man-hauling and we are already seeing the introduction of different pulks, sit-on carts and snow buggies.

Landry is passionate about kiting and considered at the top of his game.

"Flying kites on 50 metre lines (we normally fly on 25 metre lines) is as smooth as slicing through soft butter. The kite gently moves through the wind window generating consistent power. There is tremendous power but it seems to manifest itself in slow motion. As the kite descends through the power zone, I edge, carve and lean into a nice smooth right hand arc, leaning against the force of the kite. As the kite swings up through the wind window, I let it carry me up and slightly down wind. My track in the snow is similar to a downhill skier carving down a virgin slope in the Canadian Rockies When I focus on style and being at one with the kite, travel becomes hypnotic. The only other two places that offer such excellent kiting opportunities are the Greenland ice cap and Frobisher Bay in Nunavut, the latter (Iqaluit) having been home for fifteen years and the place I learned to snow kite."

Landry's love of the Poles is evident but there is a sense that if someone was to wave a magic wand he might choose something else.

"I would go on tour with the Rolling Stones as a sound technician!"

Web site: www.paullandry.ca
              www.polarconsultants.com

ERIC MCNAIR-LANDRY

"Kiting should not be put in the same class as man hauling. It's the difference between rowing across the Atlantic and sailing, there is a huge difference."

SARAH MCNAIR-LANDRY

"I think there are some neat skiing trips to do in the Arctic. Going to the North Pole at speed, very fast and very light in under 30 days with backpack and sled and when you get near the Pole ditch the sled."

It seldom follows that children walk in the footsteps of their parents but Eric and Sarah McNair Landry have done just that and then kept going, surpassing most people's triumphs in Polar adventure. Yet they are aged only 23 and 22 years respectively. Five years earlier, at the age when most teenagers are finding it difficult to get out of bed, they kited, skied and dog sledged across the Greenland Ice Cap on a 27 day 'family holiday.' This was to be a warm up for future expeditions.

Their parents, Paul Landry and Matty McNair, are two leading Polar guides, who left Ontario in the late eighties and took their small children to the cold, treeless, some might say humdrum locale of Iqaluit, on Baffin Island where for two thirds of the year the temperature refuses to rise above freezing. This most northerly city in Canada can only be reached by plane or boat when conditions allow.

By the time they were 10 years old they had learnt to ski and drive Canadian Inuit dog teams. It toughened them up, taught them a resourcefulness way beyond their tender age and gave them a love of all things white, harsh, fast and cold.

While doing my research there was an air of excitement surrounding the McNair-Landry kids. Their names kept coming up in conversation but I wasn't sure if they could add anything new or interesting. They had been described as two of the best ski 'kiters' in the world, a method of travel that allows you to cover large tracks of land (or water) at speed, attached by harness to a kite or parasail, a method first trialled by the finest Polar adventurers such as Borge Ousland and Rune Gjeldnes.

I returned to Canada and we met in Ottawa where they were visiting family. I had made a huge error of judgement. For the next several hours I was to discover that they are everything that is new and refreshing. They are the future of Polar adventure. Only a handful of adventurers could equal their successes with the professional ease with which they tackle each project and yet they don't take themselves seriously at all.

>*"Our parents instilled the ideals of adventure into us - like doing ski trails. We did downhill but not cross-country skiing. But other than dog sledging they didn't teach things like canoeing and kayaking. We were never forced into anything, oh, maybe dog sledging! Eric turns to Sarah. Do you remember that speech? 'You have no choice - you are coming out dog sledging!' Also I didn't want to wear the big baggy clothing Mom put us into!"*

Sarah is in agreement.

>*"We got a lot from our parents. Our mom designs things, she has a big industrial sewing machine because in Iqaluit you can't go out and buy anything, it is such a small town. You make your own sledges and do what you can. It's neat and it's cheaper. We have spent the winter building dog sledges and bags for the sledges and attaching snow flaps to the tents. There are a lot of things you have to play around with to make them better."*

My methodology of interviewing for the book was blown straight out of the water. I could scarcely separate their quotes. When a question was directed at one sibling, they both answered in unison, filling in each others pauses, finishing each others sentences, jousting with cracks and peppering each sentence with bursts of laughter. Their infectious interplay resembled two puppies rolling about in a basket. When I remarked on how well they seem to get on, Eric grinned.

>*"Oh yeah! We seem to get on so well! (peels of laughter) We know each other so well, but we are very direct. Curtis (Jones, the third member of their self organised expeditions) says we get on like an old couple who have absolutely no respect for each other! The way it works it that there is not much politeness involved. Politeness is just inefficient.*

>Sarah adds, *"I think it was Richard Weber and Malakhov, when they were having an argument, one would say, 'Does this get us anywhere nearer the Pole? No! You talk later. We go now!'*

>*Oh yeah! Sarah can be that regimental!"* Eric exclaims.

Eric, pin thin and 1.8 metres tall, sports a long thick ponytail of brown hair, rimless glasses and a wispy beard. He assures me that the 'bo-ho' look is as a result of laziness rather than a statement. Articulate and highly intelligent with a degree in engineering, for the past two years he 'has given up the concept of home' and he and his kites have led a gypsy life. In the last year he has travelled to New Zealand, Ellesmere, Iqaluit, America, Canada, Greenland and Iceland.

They differ in so far as Sarah likes dealing with sponsors and PR while planning for future expeditions and he, less gregarious, concentrates on the technology and web designing.

Sarah, creamy complexion, slim, yet obviously strong, with blonde, shoulder length hair and soft blue eyes spends more time kiting than her brother, on both snow and water. 'I am just better than her!' he says throwing her a teasing look. She has recently spent four months in New York studying filmmaking which she sees as her future career.

In 2004/2005 they joined their mother and Conrad and Hilary Dickinson on an unsupported expedition, Kites on Ice. The group skied to the South Pole from Hercules Inlet on the coast in 52 days, dragging their 120-kilo sledges for nine draining hours a day. It was a rite of passage for the McNair-Landry kids, Eric aged 20 and Sarah still only 18 had earned their honours in the unceasing daily slog of sledge man-hauling but they were already looking for a swifter, more radical way to travel the frozen continent.

At the South Pole they picked up a re-supply and within a day turned back on themselves, stepped into their harnesses and unfurled their kites. Swept up by the kebatic winds, they swished across the snow-packed surface, hammering over sastrugi that snatched the joints of strained legs and arms. Yet it was exhilarating and they left hundreds of kilometres in their wake. In 17 days they were back at the coast. It was an expedition marked by records and watched by everyone in the business. Sarah and her mother, who was with her, became the

first Canadian women to reach the Pole and she, the youngest person. Her brother was the youngest male. Their mother at the age of 53 was the oldest woman to reach the South Pole and Hilary Dickinson, 51, the first British woman to the South Pole and back. Interestingly, their father arrived simultaneously at the Pole having guided a British team from the other end of the continent through the Trans-Antarctic Mountains.

After the Kites on Ice performance the McNair-Landrys joined their father in a ski-kite Greenland expedition, again smashing all records by completing a crossing in seven days. Yet Sarah brushes off the records and has no qualms about denouncing one of today's greatest adventurers.

> "Borge (Ousland) has done amazing things but he had a quote in his book: something like 'if the continent had already been crossed, I don't think I would be here today.' And for me he went down a level. He has done some great trips, I am sure because he likes it too, but it's also about being the first."

In 2006 Sarah joined her father as he guided eco-activist David de Rothschild and photographer Martin Hartley in an attempt to cross the Arctic Ocean from Cape Arctichesky in Russia to Canada with 19 sledge dogs. They were airlifted over the initial 'bad' ice, annulling a 'complete traverse' record. The expedition remained on the ice for 100 days, passing 90 degrees, but as the sea ice and relationships deteriorated, happily not between father and daughter, the expedition was aborted.

> "The best part of doing your own trip is that you get to decide where you are going, what to bring and the time you are going to take to do it. For us it's just for fun but we have to get sponsorship and there is always a little bit of pressure from the sponsors."

Eric adds.

> "Records are pretty much irrelevant, even in the sponsor world. They don't care about records. For us it's not about being the first one, it's about having a good time. Records will be beaten. Eventually someone younger than Sarah will be going to the South Pole. Records are records and there are so few things you can do 'the first of' left in the Polar regions."

In 2007 they set up their own expedition called *Pittarak* (meaning fierce wind in Greenlandic) with friend Curtis Jones, a 29-year-old pharmacist. Before Sarah can finish saying. 'Curtis is the photographer and a pharmacist...' Eric butts in jokingly, much to Sarah's amusement, 'he gives us our pills, that's how we fund our trips!'

Pittarak set out to cross Greenland vertically, from South to North. It was an intrepid mission that demanded nerves of steel from the outset. They relayed 350 kilos of gear from their landing place on the coast, up a steep gully, strewn with rocks and rubble. They were forced to pick their way through a morass of mudslides before roping up to each other for safety and crossing a 29 km glacier. Struggling over glacial rivers and inching their way

around crevasses, which the pulks occasionally slid into, they eventually reached the ice cap. Eric laughs.

"Curtis kept on reminding us this was not the trip we sold him!"

It had taken four gruelling days of lugging equipment to an area safe enough to set up a decent camp and prepare their kites for take-off. Kiting demands the skill of a good skier, counter-balanced between pulk and kite. Depending on the strength of the wind kites can be as big as 17 metres wide. Sarah spells out the dangers:

"Injuries often come from crashing or getting lifted by the kite. We always wear helmets, and have different kite sizes to be able to put a smaller kite up when the winds get too strong. Yes, crevasses are also a danger when kite skiing. Another one is getting split up in a storm. When you're skiing it's easier to stay close together. But when you are flying a kite, you have to keep a little more distance, and we're travelling faster, so there is a greater chance of getting split up or losing sight of each other."

The three kiters navigated mostly by the sun, rested when the wind abated and soared across the plateau when it came up. At times their kite lines were 50 metres long with Sarah always taking the lead and Eric 'sweeping' from the back. It was vital to keep an eye on the weather and not become separated in case a snow fog as thick as pea soup might suddenly roll towards them from nowhere. The three-man team seemed to be the perfect number.

"We all do the food, we all the make the decisions. We have a democracy where if it's that person's field, for example, if it's a health issue, Curtis makes the last call. If it's about how far we should travel that day anyone has the right to refuse. It is something we have inherited from our parents but we add our own stuff."

One day, in the far-off distance and for the first time on the featureless ice cap they saw a fixed point ahead of them. Closing down on the strange shape, they discovered it was an abandoned domed United States scientific base, several storeys high, complete with satellite. Frozen in time, its rooms still filled with machinery, log books and beer bottles, they could only describe the surreal discovery

as '1980's equivalent of Walt Disney meets Star Trek."

Every expedition has an objective and for the McNair-Landry's it was to cross some 2,300 km of Greenland by harnessing the wind. It entailed hardship and danger but the message was clear, they were free spirits having a huge amount of fun and by that they hoped to inspire other young people. Was the climate change debate not something to be considered and brought to people's attention?

"We get asked this so much. With Greenland we wondered about having an emphasis on climate change and we decided 'no' because we didn't have time."

Sarah chimes in.

"We do our trips on a very low budget. We are not chartering tons of planes from location to location. For Pittarak we switched our focus to inspiring youth in adventure."

Eric continues.

"There is a whole variety of reasons to do exploration or adventure. Before, people wanted to claim (land). Today there are still some people who do it for fame and have made a living, like Will Steger. He is going with a message."

Will Steger holds the title of the greatest living explorer in his home country, the USA. His Polar expeditions began as far back as 1986 and included the 1989 Trans-Antarctic expedition with Victor Boyarsky and Geoff Somers. Today he is hailed as one of the leading environmental educators on climate change, for which he has been festooned with awards, including the Lindbergh Award bestowed on the likes of Jacques Cousteau, Thor Heyerdahl and Neil Armstrong.

Steger has asked the McNair-Landry children, and others such as Sam Branson, son of Sir Richard, to join the Will Steger Foundation to witness for themselves the floundering Polar ice caps. By inviting them on expeditions to Baffin Island, Ellesmere Island and Greenland and working with the local Inuit Steger believes passionately that with his foot soldiers and the power of the internet he can spread the gospel.

The McNair-Landry's have been responsible too for providing Steger with dog-teams and honing his skills at kiting.

> "With Will Steger, there were great expeditions but you realize it's not your dream. With Will we had specific responsibilities to fulfil but we didn't have the variables to fulfil those responsibilities, like dog training, which was very important for us. We didn't have enough time to get the dog teams we wanted; we had 30 dogs with three teams and six people and we rented a team from our mother, borrowed a team and bought another team.
>
> Will has a lot of influence. He is making a difference and he is idolized in the States. His message carries a quite a bit of weight and people are moved by him."

Then again, do they believe these expeditions are having an effect and making a difference?

> "There are 14 of us working for the foundation and they do cool stuff."

Eric agrees but voices his reservations.

> "It's having some effect. I did a lot of research before coming on to the Will Steger expedition because I wanted to know more about his points of view and global warming and I met a lot of scientists. It comes down the fact that to Will is an explorer, but is he the person you want to be receiving all you global information from? He is not a scientist. How much does he know about the science? 'Environment' gets sponsorship. Then you start getting a really mixed message about your trips. Why have you included the environment? Is it because you are going to get a specific amount of money to do the trip? On Will's expedition I had a lot of trouble with this. His major sponsor is Fagin Inc, which is an ethanol comapny, which produces green forms of gas from corn oil (bio fuels). It got a little bit sketchy. We already know that this technology is getting a lot of slack, even from the environmentalists, and hang on, whose cards are we really playing? Just because we are fighting for the opposite side does that mean that our points of view are very biased and then should we be the spokesperson? We will approach our sponsors without including global warming. We still intend to have information on global warming but it is going to be very unbiased, strictly the facts and people can believe what they choose without an opinion associated with it."

Sarah nods in agreement.

"I think it is important to have a respect for the environment and to get young people out there to start appreciating it and for them to choose for themselves to start caring for it. We did a lot of talks at school when we got back from Greenland and we can do more of that."

The reality is their passion for an extreme sport in an environment they love and want to preserve. But it comes naturally to them to encompass, to the best of their ability, a complete lifestyle with an ethos. (I discovered when trying to set up the meeting with them they had neither a car nor mobile 'phones.) On their expeditions they continue to seek the most efficient means of travel, both kinder to the environment and kinder to themselves.

"There is always room for innovation; wind turbines for energy and the big one - using solar power for heat, water and to cook with, to decrease the amount of fuel you have to bring. No one has come up with a good solution for that one yet. A lot is pretty advanced but there are always lightweight materials to be designed. The skis are as good as they are going to make them plus or minus a bit. The sled is the big one - to design a good and lightweight kiting sled that doesn't flip over."

In some cases it is difficult to separate the adventurer from the Polar climate campaigner, Many began as adventurers and have morphed into passionate activists. Undeniably those privileged to sail our oceans, cross our deserts and witness the splendour of the Arctic and Antarctic are moved enough to want to share and protect these wonderful landscapes.

   Mike Horn, Robert Swan, Will Steger and others believe that by engaging the young on expeditions they will become the future spokespeople on sustainability. The McNair-Landry's methods are similar; they too hope to inspire young people to take responsibility for the environment. And yet there is a difference, and the best I can come up with is that these future adventurers, who associate expeditions with pure enjoyment and not suffering, believe that the notion of fun is the way to channel a sense of responsibility. Eric says of his website blogs:

"We are trying to do entertaining (website) updates. We have an open email where people can write to us. The most complex thing invented is the Internet; free sharing of information and it doesn't cost you much in electricity. We are doing a trip log web site and hopefully we will get others to submit their logs with the intention of giving the general public the tips to plan their own trips. Only one team, Norwegian, had done Greenland from south to north before us, young guys in their early twenties. This year four teams went. For us it's a big success. They may not be following us but there are more doing it and that is why we would like to run a web page with the resources. For more people to get out there. What people need to realize is that change is inevitable one way or the other. We can close our eyes and pretend it's not happening but we will be forced to change. If temperatures increase we will have to move locations of certain cities and so forth."

So what of the immediate future? Sarah is booked to guide her first Antarctic expedition by ALE (Antarctic Logistics and Expeditions.) She will be leading an international group of four adventurers to the South Pole from Hercules Inlet, where all but she and one member of the team will be picked up by 'plane and flown back to base. She and her charge will kite back to the coast.

Eric is planning their next *Pittarak* expedition in 2009 with his sister and Curtis Young. They are going to kite with buggies rather than skis in the deserts of Mongolia where, he reminds you, temperatures can still fall to -30°C. After that they plan to go to Russia. For the next five years at least they will be doing expeditions.

When they can, they will return to treeless Iqaluit to finish the hut they are building from plywood scavenged from pallets and packing cases that have come off the ships. The hut, made totally from discarded materials, is already habitable with a wood burner installed. When it is finished it will have two levels and a sauna and it will be powered by solar panels and wind turbines. The eco structure can only be reached by crossing a river, the McNair-Landrys inform me, falling about with laughter, which somehow doesn't surprise me.

Each person sets out across the Arctic or Antarctic knowing they will face periods of extreme discomfort both physical and mental; to overcome those challenges brings personal fulfillment. The two young Canadians never dwell on the discomfort, it is merely a brief interloper. It is simply a means to an end and the end is having fun.

They do not forget the past explorers who forged the way; the magnificent men, Scott, Shackleton, Mawson, Nansen, Peary and others and they admire many of the modern day adventurers. They too have man-hauled and driven dogs, but by harnessing the wind, the Arctic and the Antarctic have become the McNair-Landrys playground and playgrounds are there for unbridled enjoyment. Sarah says, with her brother nodding vigorously,

> *"I think we will always go back to the Polar regions - there is a whole variety of different crossings - something like what Rune (Gjeldnes) did. Kiting is opening up all the new routes in Antarctica and in Greenland and it is bringing in a huge younger generation. Who wants to do 52 days with you head down pulling pulks?"*

Web site: www.pirttarak.com

CONRAD & HILARY DICKINSON

*"We were the first people to use snowshoes
to reach the North Pole.
We were 15 stone walking pastry cutters!"*

Conrad Dickinson and his wife Hilary are just a regular couple in their 50s, with a little extra cash which they spend on adventures. The first thing that strikes you is their no-nonsense, straight up ordinariness. Of course they are not ordinary at all, but their accomplishments are concealed by an unassuming modesty. They were the first people I interviewed for the book and I was still unsure whether to call them explorers or adventurers when Conrad joked that a Polar veteran, Geoffrey Hattersley-Smith, had once quipped 'you can explore your own arsehole with the aid of a mirror.' From then on I referred to everyone as adventurers.

Dickinson sold Dickinson Bros Ltd, a family furnishing company run by his family since 1878 and then set up Karpet Mills, a new company to provide an income to subsidise their expeditions.

What sets them apart is that their adventures are extreme, the ones you dream about (or have nightmares about, depending on which way you look at it). Where we might take a skiing holiday, this adventurous couple, who met as teenagers, have been married for 30 years and have two children, choose to ski to the South Pole, and kite back to the coast for good measure.

It was during Dickinson's time in the British Army as an officer and expert in winter warfare that he fell in love with frozen climes. In 2003, with his wife in tow, he spent their 25th wedding anniversary, and she, her 50th birthday, crossing the Greenland ice cap from east to west covering 600 kilometres.

A year later, with Matty McNair and the two McNair-Landry children, the Dickinsons left from the edge of the Antarctic continent for the South Pole. They spent one day at the Pole before unfurling their kites and hammering back across the frozen ground to the coast in

17 days. Hilary was the first British woman to the South Pole and back. I met them at their substantial Edwardian stone house in Wrexham, Northumberland. Conrad Dickinson, tall and looking somewhat underweight and drawn, had recently returned from a remarkable expedition to the North Pole with Richard Weber. Weber, considered the most experienced guide in the Arctic and venerated for his unique achievements, seemed the perfect man for Dickinson. Dickinson has the money, Weber has the knowledge. The two 'old men' chose an unsupported man-haul to the North Pole from Canada but they held another card up their sleeves: they would use snowshoes instead of skis. Hilary was not included. On her own admission she is not cut out for a sprint to the North Pole, questioning her body temperature regulation. 'If you sweat a lot, it freezes!'

The two men trained for a year before setting off, each pulling 150 kilo sledges on a journey only 10 people had succeeded in doing on skis. None had attempted the hazardous journey on snowshoes.

"I wouldn't wish a trip to the North Pole on my worst enemy! It's the hardest expedition in the world. Its colder, you start in the dusk, you have to get over the pressure ridges and then there are the currents. If you start from Canada you are on an escalator going the wrong way. At the coastal edge the ice just piles up. By contrast if you start on the Russian side it is generally first year ice and it is smoother."

There are several guides that Dickinson could have chosen to accompany him, but he tells me, in his rural Northumberland brogue:

"There are probably only about four people in the world who have got really intimate knowledge of the Arctic Ocean and probably the world's expert is Richard. He has spent more time on the Arctic Ocean than anyone else in the world. He understands how the ice works. He is modest and quiet. He had been to the North Pole ten years earlier with Malakhov and I think it appealed to him to see if he could do it without him and if he, 'the 'old guy' could still do it."

The snowshoes, with spikes underneath, worked perfectly on the rough ice and the two men made good mileage. On the flatter, more 'elastic' ice that skirts leads, skis naturally spread weight and are preferable. It wasn't long before one of the men proved the theory. They had been following a 30 metre wide lead for two hours, walking on what felt like a 'water bed' as the ocean quivered beneath their feet when suddenly it gave way.

"About day 20 it was -33°C and Richard fell through the ice but we kept going because it wasn't a good place to camp. When Richard fell in it was like one of those slow motion horror things. I took off my rucksack which was connected to my sledge. Richard was in the water and my fear was that I was going in too. I tied a rope to the back of his sledge as he clung onto the front and I pulled him out. He rolled in the snow because it's like blotting paper. Richard was calm though I think he had fear in his eyes. The general rule is: set up the tent and light up the stove. But it wasn't a clever place to camp so we walked really quickly. I was behind him and sweating. I couldn't keep up. We went on for about five hours. We then set up the tent, started the stoves and I was staggered when I picked up one of his boots. It weighed about 5 kilos (12 lbs) in weight of solid ice. His socks were frozen to the inner boot and all frozen to each other. Solid. It took three hours over two stoves to separate them. We spent six hours wringing everything out and drying his clothes, it was hard work. The next day, no big fuss, Richard said thanks for helping me. He had gauged it just right as he only had the tiniest bit of frost nip at the end of his big toe. At the end of the trip we both had a serious dunking and he got me out."

It took the men an astonishing 52 days to reach the North Pole, beating the record held by the solo adventurer, Pen Hadow, by 11 days. It was hailed as one of the great feats of present day Polar adventure by two 'old' men. As it happened it took three Norwegians to knock another three days off the same record that year.

The Canadian and Brit forfeited rest days and hauled up to 17 hours a day. The daily consumption of 7,000 calories, including an enzyme to break down fat into energy, did not prevent Dickinson losing 10 kilos. Short thickset men are built for the Arctic, not those with tall gangly frames, like his, he adds.

"I didn't want to do it solo. The polar world is a small world and too many have died. Dominick (Arduin) died. We think there was water for some 50 kilometres. She set off bravely in a canoe. The ice turns to mush and it's not firm enough to walk on and it hasn't got the fluidity to paddle in. She found herself frozen in the mush not able to paddle and not able to get out of the canoe."

Modern day adventure attracts risk takers; those who need to pit themselves against the odds and put themselves through extreme discomfort and danger. To evaluate the risk correctly, which only comes by knowing one's objective and to survive unscathed is what gives the sense of achievement and it can be addictive. Yet there is never just one reason. Hilary describes her journey to the South Pole and back:

"It's the pleasure of finding out what you can do and it's knowing very few have done it. I am not religious but it's the power of nature and we are tiny little ants. When you see huge chunks of ice coming out of the ocean you think you are so insignificant. It's pristine and unspoilt and the only way you should be there is by going under your own steam. It's a privilege to have 60 days of total isolation. It brings clarity to many of life's mysteries.
When you hit -50°C it is a totally mind-numbing experience - like being drunk. You can't think what you are going to do next. You almost close down. It takes two or three days to get used to it. You have to have physical stamina, but more important is mental stamina. You need to be able to switch off and break everything down into small components. It isn't just a physical journey it's a journey of the mind."

During the Edwardian Heroic Age there were many instances when to estimate risk was of little use. The alternative was certain death.

We handed over most of our food to the polar party (Captain Scott's party heading for the South Pole) and kept rations for four days only; thus we had to march seventeen miles a day across the plateau in order to pick up supplies at the next depot. A blizzard delayed us and we lost our direction. On January 13th we found ourselves right above the Shackleton Ice Falls, looking down on the more regular surface of the Beardmore, hundreds of feet below. A detour round the Ice Falls would have taken three days and food was short. I decided therefore to take the risk - mad in other circumstances - of tobogganing down. I can still feel the violent jolts and crashes of that wild descent and I can still see the imperturbable Crean raise his eyebrows quizzically as we leapt into the air, cleared a wide crevasse, crashed into an ice ridge, and capsized. One of my ski sticks had been torn from the sledge and I watched it roll into the blue-black chasm which had so nearly swallowed us all. I sweated to think how easily we might have shared the same fate. The gamble had come off.

The Antarctic Challenged   Admiral Lord Mountevans

Dickinson and Weber shared a close bond yet there remained an air of civility between them. Their arrival at the North Pole appeared typical of many of the men I interviewed. The women tended to sing anthems, wave flags and shed tears.

"Everything I ever asked Richard for I always said please and thank you. I felt it was a courteous thing to do and it gave a sense of normality to the very abnormal thing we were doing. We had been on the go for 18 hours when we got to the Pole and we literally shook hands. We hugged briefly for a few seconds, it was a Canadian way of shaking hands and then we said lets gets the bloody tent up. We phoned for the Russian helicopter to fetch us. It was 10 hours before they picked us up and in that time we had drifted four and a half miles."

MIKE HORN

*"I think the average human has about 30,000 days
to live. I am 40 years old.
I have about 12,000 days to live."*

It was nearly impossible to pin Mike Horn down. He did not want to be interviewed, claiming he was not a Polar adventurer, although he had succeeded in two Polar expeditions of note. He finally agreed to talk to me for an hour when I caught up with him in Cape Town, where he was visiting family.

On the designated day he strode towards me, 91 kilos of beef and brawn, his legs, clad in khaki shorts, as solid as tree trunks. Horn is of brooding good looks, dark hair, deep eyes hidden behind wrap around glasses and when he shakes your hand it feels like your fingers have been seized by Godzilla's jaw.

I enquired as to why he was missing a finger, knowing that an earlier expedition to the North Pole was aborted due to frostbitten fingers. He explained in his thick Afrikaans accent that during active service in Angola, where he served as a Commando, a mine blew up his armoured vehicle and the hatch of the vehicle slammed down, beheading a finger. It made sense; to lose a finger with frostbite seemed a little too ordinary for Horn.

We sat at a street café at the pretty Mouille Point overlooking the Atlantic Ocean and the 'one' hour turned into three. Horn is passionate, driven, intense, philosophical and unguarded, a Rambo on speed. Ideas and thoughts slam around his head as if in a pinball machine on some manic programme and spill out in a jumble of words that take some unravelling.

*"I don't belong to anywhere, I am not an Arctic explorer, what I have done no-one
else has done but I don't feel it, it's not in my heart. Even if I walked to the North
Pole backwards in the dark, which I won't do, Borge (Ousland) will stay my hero.
I am a very humble man. I got hit by nature very hard: man is nothing. I am not a
great explorer, I am just a man who wants to live my dream. All I do is put one
step in front of the other, anyone can walk! It's the attitude."*

I had come to talk mainly about his extraordinary trek to the North Pole in the darkness of winter with Borge Ousland. They were an unlikely couple. Ousland is a tall fair, slim, softly spoken, meticulous Norwegian. Horn a strapping, dark, gregarious Afrikaner, who flies by the seat of his pants.

"I am a guy who can easily adjust. I haven't got set rules when things go wrong. That is when it becomes interesting for me. Adventure is about things going wrong.

The moment you are in the storm and the ice is breaking up and the bears are around, then you have to use your knowledge for your survival. It becomes interesting. I like the survival. I like to reach into myself and take out all the bits of information inside my body.

Being afraid is my biggest asset; if I feel comfortable there is no challenge. It's not the danger I like, it's the challenge to overcome the danger and the risk."

He grew up in Johannesburg, the second of four children, but left South Africa in 1990 and now lives in Switzerland in the Vaudoise area with his wife, Cathy, a New Zealander, and two teenage daughters. To say that Horn is a maverick is clearly an understatement. His expeditions are extreme, off the wall and dangerous and he is "only interested in the things that haven't been done before."

To name but a few of these: he dropped down a 22 metre waterfall in Costa Rica with a hydro speed (basically a body board), breaking the world record for the highest descent; he traversed South America, which included descending the 7,000 km Amazon River, again on his hydro speed.

In 1999 he circumnavigated the Equator on his "Latitude Zero" expedition, without using motorized transport. During the 46,670 km he covered during the circumnavigation he endured malaria and a snake bite that left him blind for four days and he came close to drowning on Lake Victoria. In the Democratic Republic of Congo he found himself in front of a firing squad with AK47s cocked for the ready. He was only saved by the intervention of a friendly policeman. Crossing the Indian Ocean in his small boat he breasted 60 metre swells.

In 2002, turning his attention to colder climes he circumnavigated the Arctic Circle, again without motorized assistance. He named the expedition Arktos after the ancient Greek name for Arctic, meaning 'bear'. It took him two years and three months to complete the 20,000 km journey, a journey that demanded unimaginable stamina and endurance.

He walked, skied, kayaked, bicycled and sailed in temperatures that dipped to -60°C. His 14 metre aluminium boat was buffeted by icebergs and whilst camping he lost all his equipment and nearly his life when his stove blew up and the tent caught fire. He was the first person to trudge and ski across 10,000 km of Siberia.

Horn is primarily a 'solo' man with a strong character and Ousland, who is famed for his solo expeditions across the Arctic and Antarctica, although quiet, is no shrinking violet. You might imagine that their attempt as a duo to reach the North Pole from Cape Artichesky might have ended up as a clash of the Titans. Not once did either of them hint at a serious disagreement but it was not plain sailing.

"I walked around the Arctic, crossing Greenland, Canada, Alaska and Siberia, no-one has done it, that's where I acquired the knowledge. That knowledge Borge Ousland did not have, he had the knowledge of the Arctic Ocean and I didn't have that.

We walked forward for a month and the ice just drifted back and back and after a month we were back where we started and after that we had to be friends or you would just hate each other.
We were very close to the limit with the expedition. We put our knowledge together and took it to the next level. Alone we couldn't have done it.
We were both completely exposed. We knew the minute we left Cape Arctichesky no rescue was possible because no helicopter or plane can land on the Arctic Ocean once the sun is below the horizon. Once the helicopter had dropped us we were on our own, and having started, there was no going back."

Horn remembers, at the age of eleven, reading a book in Afrikaans at school about Captain Scott, with the unlikely title of *The Snow Will Always Stay White*. It was something of an epiphany and he believes it was at that point he knew he wanted to be an explorer.

"I picked it up and couldn't put it down. All I wanted to do was understand why Captain Oates gave up. I wanted to know what was going on in these guys' minds when they were in such difficulty. I wanted to go and experience what they had experienced."

However, it is with Roald Amundsen he believes he shares an unexplained affinity. Not only are they born on the same day, the 16th July, but unbeknown to Horn at the time, when he slogged through the North Western territories on his Arktos odyssey - the first person to do so alone and on foot - it was exactly a hundred years after Amundsen was the first person to navigate the Northwest Passage.

"You don't become an adventurer, you are born an adventurer. We have changed the philosophy of adventure. They went heavily dressed. You don't need warm clothes to survive the Arctic, you need to eat enough, to have enough calories to burn, to stay warm and wear light clothes so you can move faster. They went with many people, and we go alone. What they did in three years, we do in a year. I don't think there is much progress, we still can make mistakes.
Amundsen to me is one of the greatest. What we do today is for girls!"

He bursts out laughing and then apologises for the comment and I remind him that his fellow adventurer, Ousland, commented "the North Pole is for boys, the South Pole for girls, and Everest for gays!" To which he grins with approval.

It takes a fair amount of concentration to keep up with Horn's philosophical meanderings; just as you think you are beginning to grasp the gist, he veers off on another cerebral tangent.

"We (adventurers) are not running away from anything, we are running towards something. People might say 'Mike why are you running away?' For the last 15 years I have spent more time outside civilisation than in, where is my life? Is it out or in? I come back, nothing has changed. That is disappointing. When I come back

*there is more war, more problems with global warming, it's not that I don't want
to know about it, it's just that my life has different values. The colour of one's car
is not important.*

*Will I be successful one day? I haven't been successful in what I have done
because I still have to go out. Success is when you stop and you are still alive,
that is when you are successful. If you die doing what you do, then it wasn't
successful.*

*I don't exclude my family from what I do. I take them along with me. My wife is a
very strong individual, and in a way I need her more than she needs me. She does
all the planning and co-ordination but when I come back we don't talk about the
expedition"*

It is difficult to imagine exactly what would frighten Horn. He says that like all explorers,
his 'will' to stay alive is 'well developed' and the extreme risks he takes are well calculated.
That is not to say that he hasn't been within a whisker of death.

*"Most frightened? There is nothing in between life and death; a miss is as good as
a mile. There was a moment in my Arktos expedition that I stood up and fell
down, again and again, because of the wind conditions. So, I didn't want to
stand up again and I started freezing. I didn't look for the signs of the storm
coming. I wanted to walk through it.*

*You know you are close to your limit when you can't pitch your tent and you think
maybe it is easy to die. Then I thought of home. Being married and having kids is a
bonus for adventurers. People care for you and love you and you don't want to
give people the satisfaction of saying 'I told you so!'*

*I said the only way I can survive now is to turn with the wind on my back and walk
to where I came from. That was in Siberia. I know that when I go out I could die but
you must go out there with the will to win and not the fear you are going to die"*

According to Ousland, Horn was close to death as they struggled to reach the North Pole.
With three weeks still to go Horn's body was swamped by an infection, which Ousland
says was the result of frostbite. Horn brushes away the suggestion and tells me that his body,
depleted of fat reserves, was attacking muscle. Steadfastly refusing to take antibiotics, he
demonstrated a ferocious iron will which drove him forward. It surprised even Ousland,
who suggests that Horn was determined not to show any sign of weakness. Refusing
Ousland's offer to bring in a rescue helicopter, Horn capitulated on the antibiotics and
Ousland double-dosed the South African. It saved him and as the sun peaked over the
horizon heralding for the first time a new season, the odd couple limped to their goal.

*"We started running out of time. I am not a guy who cries when I hurt myself but
even when I went to the toilet in the tent and blood is coming out of your
backside… that was a body infection. I was using up muscle not body fat. We lost
30 days at the start of the expedition, we were walking forward and the ice was
pulling us back, we were many days away from the Pole but only had 30 days of*

food and fuel. We didn't have the body fat; we lost between 8 to 12 kg of weight."

Afrikaners are generally a God-fearing lot and even the smallest 'dorp' (town) in South Africa is dotted with Dutch Reform churches bulging with worshippers. Horn, you imagine, doesn't give religion much thought and would rather rely on his wits to get himself out of trouble than on some godly intervention. Yet, he is unable to reject his upbringing out of hand.

"I had to go to church but I don't go to church any more. I believe in God because I think there are times when there is something more than just luck. I ask God to give me a clear view so I can make decision. I don't think God wants me to ask for help only when I am in the shit. Like there is a hot line. I'm in the shit again, just help me! In my expeditions I am always in the shit, it's only the depth that varies. When it comes up to here (he indicates chin high) it's not comfortable, I have to stick my head up, but when it is around my knees, it smells a bit but I know I am in it."

Both men profess that by the time the expedition was over they were 'brothers' and there is no doubt they found a balance between their two forceful characters. Yet one issue they would not agree on was food. Ousland is renowned for his meticulously prepared rations, steeped in oil and fat, which Horn says brought on cramps, so they packed their own rations and watched each other warily from either end of the tent as they spooned their individual food.

Mike Horn on the Pangaea

"Børge uses a lot of fat, I use less but I use cocoa butter. Børge would take potato mash and put in olive oil. His food would be crushed up and mashed into a ball and mine would have small bits of nuts and chocolate. He took dry caribou heart. We would differ in the way that I would take two grams of coffee but he decided not to take any, so he isn't going to ask until I offer it. I would give him one gram of coffee and then he would give me a piece of chocolate. In the beginning he prepared his things and I prepared my things, in the end we shared.
There was a line in the middle of the tent. He stayed that side and I stayed this side but by the end we needed the heat from each other. It wasn't obvious, but we got closer."

Their life depended on the torches strapped to their heads that threw out a beam not much bigger than the size of a small round table. They carried 60 high-energy batteries with them, calculating they would use less battery power as it got lighter.

"We all have a sixth sense which is lost but ours came back because our lives depended on it.
Børge can work with his hands quicker than I can but his feet freeze. I can stand for hours while he has to keep moving. If you took my feet and his hands you would have the perfect explorer!"

The reticent Norwegian was not going to be drawn in by the gregarious nature of Horn, who claims Ousland believes too much talk detracts from the business in hand, but Horn, albeit with difficulty, complied.

"Børge is a man of few words and we never got into a deep conversation. I am South African, I like to speak and touch, and I'm social. When we got to the Pole we thanked each other and hugged but we were all covered up, it was -28°C. Only when I got into my sleeping bag did I live all the emotion. We stayed by the Pole for two days and when the helicopter picked us up we were already 20 km south of the Pole. We slept and we were drifting.
In the beginning I think Børge thought he would walk until Mike dies, I'll show him who's stronger, and I thought I will walk until Børge dies. When he is behind you, you can't slow down because he must work hard to follow. If you slow down he will think you are weak. Because of our competition we made it to the Pole."
I do prepare things but I like changing things. But he said to me there are three ways to do things. The right way, the wrong way and then there is MY way and I looked at him and said what about MY way?"

With this, Horn leans back in his chair, his face screwed up with laughter and orders another beer.
"I love Børge for what he is and what he has taught me."

On 22nd December 2007, the day of the winter solstice, two Russians, Matvey Shparo and

Boris Smolin, completed a full winter expedition from Cape Arctichesky to the North Pole. They arrived at the Pole on the 14th March, one week before the vernal equinox, the first sunrise. The Russians were the first to attain a true winter journey, a journey of terrifying hardship.

Ousland and Horn, on their expedition, arrived at the Pole on the 23rd March, a few days after the first sunrise. The Russians have bettered the expedition record but it remains an extraordinary accomplishment.

With little chance of rescue, the Arctic at it's coldest and the ocean at its most dangerous, it is unlikely anyone will attempt anything like this again. Except, perhaps one person.

> "I promised myself I would go back to the North Pole. Today I am thinking of crossing the North Pole at night, alone. I think it's possible because I have the experience. I don't want to be flown into Arctichesky I want to walk to Arctichesky and then walk to Canada. That would be the last thing I would do as an explorer. I have accumulated knowledge and what I must do now, I must take the next step, like the last expedition. It's all or nothing. Maybe that is a step too far."

I suggested to Horn that I wouldn't be surprised if he wasn't building some self- propelled spacecraft in his back yard. He pauses for a moment, ignores the joke, and says the only thing stopping him from going into space is money and then suddenly exploding with excitement, he launches into telling me about his next project called the 'Seven Wonders' which sounds equally outlandish. He is building a boat that over the course of the next three years will take him and a crew to Antarctica, Australia, Asia, Siberia, the North Pole, North and South America and Africa.

> "I am going to re-connect people to nature. We know about global warming but we don't speak about the resources. We have to respect the resources, so my idea is to have kids as ambassadors, talking about consuming. Kids should show kids. I am taking the kids, a couple from each country, into the elements to teach them what I know about fauna and flora and then they will communicate it. We have stopped communicating, looking people in the eye. My thought process is to get as much knowledge of all the elements as I can and take people there.
> The boat is being built and it's 35 metres long with sail. I have crossed all the oceans in the world. The first time I got into a sailing boat was when I crossed the Atlantic alone. I thought if someone else can do it why can't I?"

I wondered how Horn knew how to build a boat that would sustain the rigours of such a mammoth journey, at which he looked at me with open-mouthed astonishment.

> "Just look at an iceberg. You have to know what ice does to boats and then you have to build around that!"

A year later I discover that not only had the indomitable Horn overseen the building of the boat in Sao Paulo, on funds that appear to have been scraped together on a wing and a prayer, but that the expedition, re-named Pangaea - the ancient Greek word for 'all earth,' - has set sail from it's berth in South America. The revised four year journey covering 100,000 km, or what Horn typically calculates on his website is 2,103,840 minutes, is heading for Monaco to be 'baptised' by Prince Albert of Monaco.

As the sun starts to dip and Table Mountain looks more magnificent than ever, Horn stands to leave. He looks at me grinning and shrugs his shoulders.

"People say why are there so many obstacles in life. Me? I don't wish for FEWER obstacles!

Web site: www.mikehorn.com
Books: Conquering the Impossible: My 12,000mile Journey around the
                   Arctic Circle
               Objective: The North Pole by Night
               Latitude Zero
               A l'ecole du Grand Nord

P.S. In July 2008, Horn brought the beautiful 35m Pangaea down the River Thames in London and into St Katherine's Dock for a press conference. An extraordinary feat in itself.

ROBERT SWAN OBE

"Where I think things have gone wrong with Polar exploration or adventuring is that it's here today and gone tomorrow. That is the essence which drives me, that all this effort goes to self-masturbatory exercise. I walked to the Poles but what does it mean?"

By the time I have finished interviewing Robert Swan I am punch drunk. The powerfully built, barrel chested, Briton, with ice blue eyes and with more than a hint of extreme good looks still showing on his weather-beaten face, is wearing shorts and T-shirt on a particularly wet and gloomy English autumn day. He greets me warmly at his comfortable modern apartment that belongs to his (second) wife, he is quick to inform me, and which looks out upon the Thames in Greenwich, London.

You don't get to ask too many questions because Swan is telling you how it is. He is on a mission, an all-out global mission on climate change awareness and the preservation of Antarctica. Whereas Al Gore's platform is built on political clout Swan's podium is founded on 'the first man in history to reach both Poles.'

He dances around on his feet, metaphorically speaking that is, fists up, verbally throwing punches and jibes at more or less everything that comes up in conversation. It's nigh impossible to get a word in. He is on you like a flash. Yet, he also manages a charm offensive, so I try not to take anything too personally.

By the time I leave it feels as if I have watched Muhammad Ali fight twelve rounds in the ring. Swan dances like a butterfly and stings like a bee.

"I don't like the word explorer and I find the word adventurer irritating because we are not either of those things. I would say that what I have learnt is that the last great exploration, actual adventure, left on earth, is not idiots like me walking to the Poles, it is to survive on earth as a species. The world won't collapse. We are in the process of blowing it up. So that is what I have learnt over 25 years of doing these things." He pauses then relents: *"So if the word exploration or adventure is used then I am happy as it has to be an exciting thing to survive on earth. I suppose I started all of this, this adventurer bit!"*

He is from a middle class family, public school and university educated and the youngest of seven children, which goes some way to explaining why he needs to be heard. He who shouts the loudest…

In 1979, about the time Ran Fiennes set out on his Transglobe expedition, he set out to raise $5 million dollars to fund an expedition to the South Pole. In those days adventurers were soundly dissuaded from embarking on expeditions in Antarctica. No country with scientific bases wanted the responsibility and expense of rescuing errant 'explorers'. Swan went on to fulfil their worst fears.

It took five years to raise the money, but in 1984, at the age of 33, Swan realized a dream he had nurtured since a small boy - 'to follow in the footsteps of Captain Robert Falcon Scott.' He bought a 36.5 metre trawler, made a few alterations to it, named it *Southern Quest* and persuaded 25 volunteers, including Dr Mike Stroud, to join him and set sail down the Thames to Antarctica via New Zealand. The expedition stretched over three years and included overwintering on Ross Island.

> "Antarctica is a natural reserve land for science, not adventurers and explorers or people who call themselves that. It was right, how could a government help someone who wants to walk to the Pole. They said no! The only way to do it was the way we did it and that is why no one had done it since Scott or Shackleton. Who was stupid enough to live for seven years in a warehouse here (he points across the river) raising millions of dollars to do it?"

This journey was truly in the footsteps of Scott, or at least it began in the steps of Scott and ended more in the footsteps of Shackleton when Southern Quest, crushed by the ice, sank, just like Shackleton's ship Endurance.

> "I must be very, very clear that more people had stood on the moon than walked to the Pole when I did it. I was the first person in history to walk to both Poles, North and South. So in a strange way I started all of this. I respect all the people (who have done it since) I have no problem with that, but we were the only people since Scott, Shackleton, Amundsen and Mawson. In the 1970s no one was doing it."

Just when one is resigned to the fact that self-promotion and self-importance are the nature of the beast of leaders of expeditions to the Poles, Swan wins one over.

> "I wasn't doing it for the environment - I was doing it because it went down with girls at parties and to be somebody. I had studied history (Durham University). I wanted to make my piece of history just once.
> This had to do with respect. I saw a film, Scott of the Antarctic with Johnny Mills. That film inspired me to go to Antarctica, to walk to the South Pole and to follow in the footsteps of Scott and Shackleton for real. So my only option to get to Antarctica was to buy a ship and sail right past here, (he points at the river) live for a year in Antarctica as they did and then walk to the Pole. We did the crack, it was the only way you could get to Antarctica and it cost millions of dollars.
> I am very happy to say now I have no interest in the doing of it. I hate it. I can think of a thousand better things to do with my life than be cold and live in tents with smelly men, not get laid for a year. I can think of a lot better things to do with my life than Polar travel. It's not nice but it was my dream."

Swan freely admits he lacks all the skills required to survive in Polar regions. You might say he is the antithesis of Børge Ousland.

> *"I have no interest when people ask me to test clothing and equipment and I send it back in the post. Can I put up a tent? Not really! A stove? No! Mend a sledge? No! No! I am good at raising finance to do things that are a bit odd. I am not a good leader but I am extremely good at selecting people and I get the best. So on the ship the captain got us there. In Antarctica, Gareth Wood, our brilliant engineer, was in charge of the hut and we listened to him and when we started walking, we had one of the finest Polar travellers and mountaineers that this country has never recognised, Roger Mear, and we had Mike Stroud as our base doctor."*

The expedition set off in January 1984 on a 27,400 kilometre journey to Ross Sea Island stopping off at Lyttleton, New Zealand to meet Bill Burton, the last surviving member of Scott's fatal expedition. Arriving in Antarctica and setting up base within the area of Scott's old hut at Cape Evans, Swan, with his team of John Tolson, Mike Stroud, Roger Mear and Gareth Wood saw the Antarctic winter out. By the end of November of that year Swan, Mear and Wood set out on a man-hauling slog to the South Pole leaving Stroud and Tolson to hold the fort.

In the meantime *Southern Quest* deposited a Twin Otter onto the ice which was going to be piloted by the legendary Antarctic pilot, Giles Kershaw. Tragically, Kershaw was later to die in a gyrocopter accident and his Scottish wife, Anne Kershaw MBE, took over the company Adventure Network International which today is ALE and the only company to service adventurers from Punta Arenas to their base, Patriot Hills, in the Antarctic.

As the men completed their 1,400km trek to the South Pole the longest unsupported expedition at that time, the *Southern Quest* was caught in the grip of pack ice and sank. The three adventurers were informed by the Americans based at the Pole that the Twin Otter would no longer be coming for them.

> "Our ship sank. We were told to abandon Antarctica, leave our hut, chuck our plane. Why did we lose our ship? There were all kinds of things. Giles Kershaw, aviator extraordinaire, had arranged for a DC 3 with himself at the wheel, to fly from South America to the South Pole to collect us there. That is why we had our passports. This would allow Southern Quest to come into McMurdo when the ice was out and pick up Stroud and Tolson at our base when it was safe from ice."

According to Swan, the company that owned the DC 3 were told that if they let Kershaw pilot the plane to collect Swan and his team at the South Pole it would lose its contracts to charter for the National Science Foundation. This would force the expedition to rely on the goodwill of the Americans to be rescued, proving that private expeditions were to be discouraged at all times.

> "But our team said 'sod that', bought a plane and put it on Southern Quest but she had to go south early and she was Ice Class Three and not really suited for it. We couldn't arrive at the Pole and ask the Americans for a hitch back home. We would have lost. So the ship comes in early, unloads Giles and the aeroplane ready to fly to the Pole, job done. Ship tries to get out, is caught by the ice, sinks. Giles is ready to fly to the Pole, engines turning over and the British government tells him not to. Shackleton lost his ship and we have to take a ride with the Americans to base camp.

The Americans then flew the three men back to New Zealand

> I said 'what about clearing up all our stuff?' They said 'leave it' and I said 'sod you, we are not going to leave three people here for another year.' I take the ride with the Americans and they send me a bill for 80,000 dollars!

The American Coast Guard had plucked the beleaguered Southern Quest crew off the pack ice with helicopters and deposited them at McMurdo base and finally flew them back to New Zealand.

Greenpeace offered to collect the three men stranded at their base and at the same time remove their rubbish. However, ice conditions prevented them from doing so.

> "I have three people stuck on the base and I am fighting for some dignity. So I get hold of Giles and we fly from South America in a Twin Otter plane all the way to McMurdo Sound. It's a nightmare and I had to go to the Chilean government and say, you helped Shackleton; help me to get my people out.

Giles and I fly across the whole continent, pick up the three people, fly across Antarctica to South America, land, and there is a telephone call from the Greenpeace ship saying the ice has gone and we are coming in after all. We did leave Antarctica tidy and sod the Americans! That gives you some idea of what Shackleton, Scott, Mawson and I - and I am not in that bracket - have to face. Flying from Punta Arenas to the Pole and flying out, that is a whole different game. I feel proud of what we did, especially finishing it off with a bit of style.

I was the first to do it and no one can take it away from me. I am damn proud of it, not what I did but what we did. We did it radically differently. We carried no radio communication to the South Pole because we did justice and respect to the real explorers.

We had nothing. Even Borge (Ousland) won't go anywhere unless in eight hours there is a message on some satellite beacon to tell everybody where he is. We were into the history of it and we felt we had the chance to touch the isolation and commitment of Shackleton and Scott. It's a whole different game."

Swan was left with mounting debts but he was not nearly finished. The South Pole debacle had taught him one thing and that was that he could rise above the seemingly impossible.

Three years after reaching the South Pole, for which he received the Polar Medal, he pulled together a team of eight people from seven nations, including the great Russian explorer, Mikhail Malakhov, and set out for the North Pole on an expedition called *Ice Walk*. If that wasn't enough he deposited 22 young people from 15 nations at the base camp at Eureka on Ellesmere Island and produced educational films. These outreach programmes with modern technology are commonplace today, but then it cost thousands of dollars and the concept was way before its time.

The North Pole was bagged and Swan became the first person in history to walk to both Poles. Yet he was left in a bad place.

"It was a feeling of disappointment. You had bust your butt big time and it hadn't meant anything to anybody and it was like you had spent hours getting everything right and you gave interviews and then you picked up the paper and it's nothing like you have said.

I was very messed up and drank a lot. I was disillusioned. I did it at this massive level and owed all this money and my back was messed up."

It comes as a bit of a surprise to discover, at that low time, Swan had an epiphany, but that is what makes him so engaging. At the bottom of a glass held to his lips, he saw the figures of his heroes.

"I saw them very clearly at the bottom of a glass. Shackleton, Scott, Amundsen. All their faces looking at me, laughing, saying 'Rob welcome to the real expedition. You have walked to the Poles but now join the real one. If you do all this shit you will go into massive debt, because that is the only way to do it. Then you have to live for the rest of your life in debt. Pioneers like us have to push it out so far to

make it happen, borrow money and end up in debt. You think you have finished.
You have just begun: it's just begun matey!'
I have been virtually bankrupt since I walked to both Poles 20 years ago. I am
cracking on a bit now. I had done both Poles by 33, now I am 52 and I hope I
don't end up a pauper."

Yet Swan didn't run out of steam. If anything, after his Pole exploits, he felt driven, on a crusade to make people not just aware of climate change but to do something about it.

"I came back from the South Pole with my face hanging off, my eyes all burnt out.
I said we have just walked under a hole in the ozone layer and without the ozone
layer nothing is going to grow on earth and no-one listened. They do now."

Making people want to protect Antarctica, 'the last great wilderness on Earth,' might prove that there is a vestige of hope in them - wanting to slow down global warming. Swan knew he had two things to do. Use his exceptional talent as a public speaker to inspire and raise cash and to embrace the young, the planet's future custodians. Supported by Jacques Cousteau and Sir Peter Scott, son of Captain Robert Scott and Founder of the World Wildlife Fund, Swan began his mission. He set up an organisation called 2041.

In 1961 the Antarctic Treaty was signed by 44 nations, to ensure Antarctica would be used for peaceful purposes and its fragile environment protected. The Madrid Protocol provides extra additional protection including the ban on mining or mineral exploration. In 2041 the moratorium expires; about the time it is predicted the coal reserves will have nearly run out in the rest of the world.

"I have spent 22 years now with 2041. I drive the whole bloody thing and I have
the best person in the world to help me, Anne Kershaw." (Wife of the late Giles
Kershaw)

Swan's programmes over the years are staggering. He was a keynote speaker at the Rio de Janeiro 1992 Earth Summit. The following year he took 35 young people from 25 nations to Antarctica. It was the start of an enormous waste removal exercise over many years - 1,500 tons from the Russian base, Bellingshausen. He then took on the World Summit for Sustainable Development in Johannesburg in 2002, and took the 2041 sail boat on an overland voyage throughout South Africa. He joined up with the charity 'LoveLife' and spread the word on Aids awareness.

Each year he takes a group of up to 70 international people, the movers and shakers of industry and business, to Antarctica where they see for themselves the importance of the 'last great wilderness on Earth.' It is perhaps the greatest of his strategies. No-one can help but be moved by Antarctica. Those who have attended his lectures and those he has engaged in his projects talk of Swan in reverent terms. He has driven the message home.

"I am not a campaigner, I am a catalyst. I have never been an explorer and would
hate to be called an adventurer. I have taken 500 people to Antarctica to clear

1,500 tons of rubbish because we are trying to protect it. So to inspire people you have to do something that cost six million quid, which I had to raise. It took 11 years to achieve. It took young people from so many nations to help do it and to encourage people to use renewable energy, because for some reason we are sitting on our backsides not being able to see what is happening. But they go away as champions. I have people I took to the Arctic and Antarctic who were 18 but are now 40 - that's depressing. They are now serious players doing some good stuff."

Having cleared away the rubbish, Swan set up an 'E-Base' on the scientists abandoned station on Bellingshausen. It was to be the world's first educational base in Antarctica to run wholly on sustainable energy; to prove that if it can be done in Antarctica it can be done anywhere in the world.

We touch on a subject that makes Swan apply a few heated body punches - using climate change as a platform to launch expeditions, often a successful way to raise funds.

"Will Steger is a great man. I have total respect for him. Mike Horn? It's fine what he's doing but what is irritating is that people jump onto it to keep themselves in the adventure spotlight and it's selfish. They are not giving much. Mike Horn has done some amazing stuff but people view it in simple terms - he has jumped on the band-wagon to keep himself in adventure. I don't think he has jumped on it with much integrity.
Some of these people drive me nuts, we were doing this 20 years ago and they should have moved on!
Ran Fiennes. He was a great pioneer; he was out there just doing it. I like him and respect him, good on him. Another person I truly respect in the game is Børge Ousland. Børge just does it to do it.
I don't give a shit what people think about me but what I give a shit about is that we are in an emergency. I am the engine - I am not afraid of anyone, except myself - get that straight!" He says with a grin.

Swan's mission is wind driven much of the time, as he sails from continent to continent in his *Voyage for Cleaner Energy* sailing ship; its sails made from recycled plastic bottles, its energy run on wind turbines and bio-fuels. Each stop is punctuated by lectures heard by thousands of young people and given to corporate giants such as BP, Nokia, HP Credit Suisse etc.

"We have 10 years to sort this out and I will give my all for another two years before I blow up. There is only one reason that you are sitting here - because I walked to both Poles; because it happens to be a special story. It still is the thing I am very proud of. It showed me how to raise money. I raised over 50 million dollars for everything I have done and that is funding I have put together for educational programmes. I have been very forceful with you because it's a different game now. Do it like Borge (Ousland) but don't play at it, don't feed off the environment just to keep your adventure going."

Like all great fighters Swan gives me a bear-hug just before I leave the ring. He tells me it has been an exhausting year with constant lecturing and travelling, surviving for weeks on his E-Base on Antarctica and, not that he admits it, something he is quietly proud of - bearing the 2008 Olympic Torch through St Petersburg in Russia.

There is no doubt he is a champion and like all champions he refuses to be bowed.

"We would go to Antarctica to destroy and ravage it, to get fossil fuels. By not using fossil fuels we won't go there to destroy it. If we can preserve Antarctica we might save the planet because as Sir Peter Scott said on his death bed, Rob, tell the people to have the sense to leave the place alone."

Web site: www.2041.com
Books: In the Footsteps of Scott
              Destination: Antarctica
              Ice Walk

RUNE GJELDNES

"It was a big labyrinth; no one had been up or down the Priestley Glacier before, never. I got a warning from glaciologists that they would not recommend it because of the crevasses and the strong winds and hurricanes down there."

When I met Rune Gjeldnes in the Grand Hotel in Oslo it was exactly a year to the day that he had set off alone and unsupported across Antarctica. We clinked our beer bottles in celebration but there was an air of vulnerability about him. He had achieved one of the greatest journeys in Polar history and had made it look easy. Yet, something was amiss with the stocky, bright eyed, 37 year old Norwegian, sporting a goatee beard that made him look like a woodland mythical creature.

The youngest of four brothers, he was a nervous child. Many things had frightened him, including the dark. Fortunately by the time he reached 16 years of age his insecurities disappeared and he began to dream about becoming an adventurer. Which is how most things start for Gjeldnes, turning his dreams into a reality.

He joined the SEALS, the Norwegian Naval Special Command, as did another great Norwegian adventurer, Børge Ousland. Thus started the lessons on planning and preparation and, above all, the feeling that failure was not an option.

It was in the SEALS that he met his fellow adventuring partner, Torry Larsen, with whom he crossed Greenland, followed by the only unsupported crossing of the Arctic Ocean, which nearly cost them their lives.

Larsen is a tall strapping 1.95 metres, towering over the short and stocky Gjeldnes. Their friendship, Gjeldnes claims, was the most important factor of their success.

Their ethos that everything depended on your partner's state of mind and body and that you would work within the limits of whoever was the weakest on the day and not the strongest, was a key to their success. This simple but often unheeded recipe is what cemented an extraordinarily close bond and led to their ultimate success.

On the 16th February 2000 Gjeldnes and Larsen set off to be the first to cross the Arctic Ocean unsupported, from Siberia to Canada. The 1,914 km crossing was considered to be one of the greatest challenges attempted in Polar history.

After 109 days of relentless hardship the men staggered into Cape Discovery carrying only a few belongings on their backs. For the last four days, having run out of food and fuel and with no sleep, they had no choice but to push on towards the pick-up point. By the time they reached the Canadian coast Gjeldnes had lost 21 kilos in weight, Larsen 35 kilos; a doctor pronounced them only a few days from death.

At the start of the expedition, which was sponsored by SEALS and monitored by them for scientific research, they were deposited by helicopter 16 km inland from Cape Artichesky. In the murky tail end of winter it would be nine days before the sun's rays appeared above the horizon. Joined by the border patrol guards, the helicopter crew gave them a farewell dinner of reindeer soup and shots of vodka. With Russian flamboyance, the party proceeded to fire off AK47s as a farewell fireworks display.

Finally the helicopter disappeared into the dusk and it would be more than three months before the two Norwegians would see another human being. Ahead of them lay 2000 km of frozen ocean, continuously in motion, an ice sheet, growling and breaking, a morass of pressure ridges, ice rubble and open channels of water.

Each man hauled two sledges, total of 200 kilos, forcing them to relay their sledges over the broken terrain. They found themselves facing leads of inky blue water, sometimes many metres wide and stretching as far as the eye could see, forcing them to turn directly east or west. Just as easily the leads would freeze over, forming the flat surfaces every sledge hauler prays for yet always posing the risk of being too thin to travel on.

North Pole nightmare

The back-breaking work finally forced them to abandon a sledge each. They packed what they could into two sledges and carried the rest, 25 kilos each, in rucksacks on their backs. *'I've been full of hatred'* wrote Gjeldnes in his diary. *'A terrible ordeal, even worse than I'd thought possible. Every step was painful.'*

Sledge hauling in the Arctic has been described as 'dragging a dead horse over an earthquake zone'. On one day alone, they drifted helplessly as the currents swept them 24 km off course.

Larsen showed moments of vulnerability, admitting to feeling terrified when his fingers were too cold to fasten his down vest and he had to rely on Gjeldnes to help him. 'What if your fingers had been the same?' he asked his friend.

Approaching the North Pole they met yet another impassable lead. Refusing to be hampered again by having to take a course due east, they found an ice flow on to which they clambered and ferried themselves across the 20 metres of water singing all the way.

"A lot of the time there was a good mood between me and Torry; it is really enjoyable being out with him except I snore and he hates snoring!"

Finally, nearly two and a half months later, they arrived at the North Pole, giving a huge boost to their spirits, and they lit up cigars in celebration. Unlike most adventurers Gjeldnes is partial to cigars, snuff and cigarettes.

"The scientists on the projects have been eager to find out if smoking is terrible for me on expeditions, compared to the people who don't smoke. They have found nothing and I know its not healthy but mentally it is very healthy. I would not have gone across Antarctica without it. It's an important mental part of my life. If you meet a problem it is so nice to sit down and relax and finish the cigarette. Then you have solved the problem and instead of jumping around you just calm down."

The euphoria of reaching the Pole was brought quickly into check on realizing that at the rate they were moving they simply did not have enough food and fuel to last them to the end. If conditions had been bad since leaving Siberia, they only got worse as they battled towards Canada.

During the 1907 Nimrod expedition, Shackleton, with three of his men, Marshall, Adams and Wild, dragged sledges for some two and half months towards the South Pole. Frost-bitten and half-starved they realized the Pole was beyond their reach. Their meagre rations would not sustain them to the Pole and back. They set up camp at 88 degrees. Here they left their sledges and taking a camera, the Queen's flag and lunch stuffed in their pockets, they half ran and half marched for seven hours before planting the flag - ninety-seven miles from the South Pole.

Exhausted by their efforts the homeward journey of 700 miles nearly cost them their lives. It is one of the greatest stories of human courage and endurance in Polar history.

As the spring thaw set in, leads continually opened. At times the ice was just a few centimetres thick and it was only by keeping up a forward momentum that they were prevented from falling through into the ocean with no chance of rescue. The pressure ridges towered above them, sometimes 15 metres high, cutting their daily distances to a mere eight kilometres a day. Doubts started to creep in.

They had one option - to dump the sledges and pack the maximum they could carry into their rucksacks, and make a dash for the Canadian coast. It would mean nine-hour shifts covering 28 km (15 miles) a day over a 19-day period. It was a brave but perilous decision. Not only would they lose their 'rafts' to cross open water but also the weight they were each personally carrying would increase their chances of falling though the ice.

The determination not to fail forced Gjeldnes and Larsen to take equally desperate measures.

"We knew when we got the idea it would be dangerous crossing thin ice and also if we met lots of water we could not cross it. We were living in uncertainty. After some days working with backpacks we got used to it, but we always had that uncertainty. We knew if we came to open water we would fail. We had people back home sitting on the ice map but they didn't tell us anything about it (open water) they didn't want to worry us - they could see it on satellite."

Rune Gjeldnes North Pole Traverse – Running out of time

The men were caught in a maelstrom of moving ice as they inched their way forward, often having to take off their skis and crawl on all fours. Geldnes described it as a mountain range of ice blocks. Physically they were exhausted. Gjeldnes complained of an infected Achilles heel and the rucksack rubbed Larsen's protruding hipbones. Cracks began to show in their mental state brought on by the ever-present fear of falling through the ice.

> *"One day I suggested to Torry we should plan a resupply just in case. He was almost angry; 'if we start planning that, we will fail.' Some days you feel enough is enough and you know when you come into the tent everything will be okay. We were doubtful we would have success but we didn't think about giving up."*

Amundsen's 1910 dash to the South Pole

Unjustly, in 1910 Fredrik Hjalmar Johansen was left at base camp during Amundsen's successful flight to the South Pole as punishment for berating Amundsen for incompetence in front of his men. Earlier, Amundsen had ignored Johansen's advice and set out too early for the Pole in his eagerness to beat Captain Scott. He was forced to return to base camp but ignored the plight of his men whom he left to fend for themselves in -60 degrees without a tent or a stove to melt snow for water. Johansen carried his fellow team member, Kristian Prestrud, who was close to death from the cold, to the base where he confronted Amundsen. Amundsen had his men sign a paper agreeing that only he could write about the expedition, thus silencing them. Johansen, who had also contributed so courageously to Nansen's survival in the Arctic, committed suicide at the age of 45

While crossing a flow Gjeldnes gingerly stepped from one block of ice to another. Suddenly he heard the ice crack beneath him and he slipped slowly into the ocean. Gripping onto a block of ice he felt the water rise above his knees. He clung frantically on to the ice and screamed for Larsen, terrified the ice supporting his upper body would not hold and that the current would sweep him away or that he might be crushed by another piece of floating ice. His cries went unheeded; Larsen had his earphones plugged in. Then he himself fell. The weight of his rucksack threw him with such force onto the ice he was unable to breathe, believing he had broken his breast bone.

 Shaking with cold, Gjeldnes decided his best hope was to remain as still as he could. Only the buoyancy of his rucksack, containing all his supplies critical for survival and the precious camera, kept him afloat.

> *"It's hard to say if I would have got out (alone). When you fall into the water you are worried but if you are alone you are in a different mental attitude so you are more prepared to help yourself. It's possible to get up but I felt stuck. You don't worry about the equipment on your back getting wet when you are alone.*
> *When one thing goes wrong something else happens as well there is always a chain reaction - you should be very careful in such situations."*

Eventually, Larsen got back on to his feet and turned back. Instead of dragging his partner out of the morass he asked for the camera, fortunately still dry on top of the rucksack, in order to record the ensuing drama! Gjeldnes was in the water for 10 minutes.

With 30 km to go and very little food and fuel left, just enough to melt water, they agreed to push on, stopping only for sips of liquid. Sleep was out. The terrain, fields of ruptured ice, was the worst they had encountered during the whole trip.

Finally rations, except for chewing gum and cough drops, ran out and they had no means of melting ice for drinking water. They stumbled on, dehydrated and sleepless over chaotic ice boulders, hardly able to put one foot in front of the other, when suddenly they heard the engine of a Twin Otter aeroplane above them. The pilot had spotted them, two lonely figures on an ice flow the size of a football field and surrounded by water. There was nowhere for the plane to land, it banked and disappeared back into the clouds. Gjeldnes broke down with exhaustion and frustration and then within minutes smiled at the absurdity of the situation.

There was nothing for it but to try and cross the several-hundred-metre-wide lead that surrounded them. For several more hours they bunny hopped from ice flow to ice flow, zig-zagging precariously towards land. Suddenly in the distance they made out the black shape of the plane. It had landed and a group of figures was coming to meet them. Larsen and Gjeldnes were close to death but they had made it to the coast. Their record is yet unbeaten.

At our first meeting Gjeldnes and I talked mainly about his crossing of Antarctica. It had been done before by others, including his compatriot Børge Ousland, who traversed Antarctica solo in 1995 from Berkner Island to McMurdo. But Gjeldnes covered a further distance from the Russian base of Novolazarevskaya in Dronning Maud Land to Terra Nova Bay. It was an expedition of heroic proportions and it held the Polar community in awe.

He was the only man to complete both traverses, the North and South Pole, without resupplies. Børge Ousland's feat of both traverses was no less awe inspiring but he was forced to have a new sledge brought in when his original sledge broke in the early stages of his Arctic crossing, classifying his expedition as resupplied. Such is the way of Polar records.

Gjeldnes at times made the journey look easy. He hauled, kited and skied the distance in 90 days, yet the laurels did not come without cost. To begin with I couldn't quite put my finger on what it was about this young Norwegian that I found troubling. The words tumbled haltingly from his lips. Was it his broken English I wondered? As the story unfolded he would fast forward to the last days of the expedition and then, as if remembering the fear, he would divert my attention to other incidents on the expedition.

He reproached himself for losing a ski when it fell off the back of his sledge while kiting. It was a disaster as skis spread the weight and minimise the risk of falling through the snow bridges that span crevasses. He had the treacherous Priestley Glacier, with its maze of crevasses, ahead of him and he was doused in fear.

The Priestley Glacier, named after Raymond Priestley, the geologist on Scott's ill-fated 1911 expedition, is a 94 km labyrinth of ice and fissures that drops down from the plateau to the coast. No-one in history had made the perilous descent and Gjeldnes had been warned by scientists that it would be folly to do so.

The Priestly Glacier

"Don't ask me how I lost my ski, it was in the morning when I took a break. After two hours, I realized my ski was gone and I had already done 40 km. It was not a good idea to walk back. I was furious because you are not allowed to lose a ski"

At the beginning of the expedition Gjeldnes' sledge fell into a crevasse nearly pulling him with it. Eighteen days into the expedition he ignored his freezing feet and one of his worst fears became a reality: two toes on each foot turned black with frostbite. It became a constant reminder that it could end his hopes of success.

"Frostbite definitely frightened me. If you don't have enough self-discipline you get it. I got it early on in the trip, on day 17. You know it's going to be a problem, so every hour for most of the rest of the trek I was moving my toes all the time. You are concerned with the uncertainty, you never know what will happen the next hour or the next day: this is torture. Uncertainty on an expedition is the big challenge. It kills the enjoyment. Frostbite is painful mentally as well as physically; if you don't keep moving the frostbite will go deeper. I didn't get blisters, my skin just went black."

Eventually he brought the conversation back to the Priestley Glacier, until finally it was as if the sluice gates of terror had been opened. Gjeldnes sounded like a haunted man and equally disturbed as to why the glacier had brought on this reaction when he had been in critical situations before.

"I was alone for a long time and the Priestly Glacier did something to me. I have never been so afraid of dying as during the five days on the glacier. Never. This fear of death was so strong. It was not for a moment, it was for five days, it was constant."

As we sipped our beers, tucked away in a quiet corner of the famous Oslo hotel, he was at pains to tell me he was not himself. He had been back from the Antarctic for nine months and was looking forward to moving to a new house with his fiancé, Aina, and yet things did not sit easily with him.

"I am not back again, especially with meeting other people and taking the telephone, writing emails. I was alone for a long time. It was close to being in a war zone, I was thinking about that when I was up there and afterwards. I knew if I was too late [going down] the glacier, I would get really strong winds and if I hurry too much I could easily fall into a crevasse. It was mainly the crevasses, it was a labyrinth from 1-15 metres wide with snow bridges I had to cross."

Gjeldnes did descend the glacier without terrible mishap though he lost his digital camera containing 500 photographs. As he lay on his stomach on a ridge it slipped out of his pocket, slid over the lip of the crevasse and into the void. He fastened two bolts, secured a rope and started to descend into the abyss. Instinct told him to draw back. 'It was the saddest thing that happened to me during the whole expedition.' He would be unable to share the memories.

It took him 90 days to cross Antarctica. He has sailed, skied, man hauled and teetered on the edge of death; he took a route that no man had taken before and it is unlikely anyone will follow him.

Four months after our interview I telephoned Gjeldnes to get an update on how he was feeling.

"I feel better, definitely, because I have moved (from Oslo to Trondheim) and I am getting control back. I am being more social. We are still there, not opening emails and talking to people, but it is much better. I have been in critical situations before but this is the first time alone. It took four years to plan it and suddenly it was done. I don't have any good answers why it was worse this time."

Web site: www.rune-gjeldnes.com
Books: Beyond the Poles
              Dead Men Walking

ANN DANIELS

"They popped us on the ice.
I thought this is the start of my fantastic dream.
I was elated but I was also terrified."

On meeting Ann Daniels nothing appears too out of the ordinary. Of medium height, medium build, a mother of four children, she lives in a semi-renovated house, the garden strewn with toys, in an ordinary village in Somerset in England. Then she starts to talk and suddenly she is firing on all cylinders, a little dynamo, crackling with energy.

From a working class family, she grew up in Bradford in the north of England, the youngest of five children, and she attributes her feisty character to having to compete with four older brothers. She left school at 16 and started working in a bank.

"I went to a normal comprehensive school and I wanted to go to university but with my background there was not a chance! My father said university is for long-haired layabouts. You get a job and bring some money home! I had a really good brain; I got nine 'O' levels and an A in maths. I didn't do 'A' levels because I didn't think I was good enough. But that was a lesson learnt because I was good enough. My expectations were I would work, get married, have a family and go back to work."

And that is more-or-less what happened. She married a man in the Services and settled down to have a family. However, unable to conceive naturally she opted for IVF treatment and to her surprise she found she was pregnant with triplets. Gaining a massive 56 kilos in weight during her pregnancy did not dampen her spirits.

When the two girls and a boy arrived, Daniels discovered she was a natural problem solver as well as practical, the two traits she was going to need as one of Britain's best women Polar adventurers; not that she knew it at the time.

"Life was manic. I found out the first night if you fed them one after the other, by the time you put them down you didn't get any sleep, so I fed them all at the same time. I would put one on each breast and bottle feed the third and put them down and be very strict. I was determined to enjoy it and I did. I learnt I could achieve anything."

When the triplets were 18 months old her husband showed her an advertisement seeking 'ordinary' women for an all female relay team to the North Pole.

"I had never had a rucksack on my back or walked further than the garden path. I filled in the application and included £75, so much money then. I thought I was going to be one of those gullible women who send money to something and never see it again."

A kit list arrived with instructions for the first day's selection organised by the British Polar adventurer Pen Hadow, the first person to walk solo and unassisted to the North Pole from the Canadian coast. More than two hundred women applied. Daniels borrowed everything from her husband's friends, mostly ex-military, and arrived on Dartmoor looking like someone from the Special Forces.

"Everyone was scared of me! They tramped us around Dartmoor in army style - it was horrendous! I was out of my league; my rucksack was made for a Royal Marine and hung off my shoulders. Sixteen hours later it was dark and raining and I cried but I thought this is my door in life to do something special and I am not going to give in."

The women were told they would be called back in nine months time for a four-day session of boot camp. Daniels had nine months to get into shape and spent every waking hour and most of her babies' sleeping hours, training.

She returned for the final test on Dartmoor, honed and fit, and able to read a compass and map. At the end of the final selection her name was called out. She had passed the test and with 19 other women, the 1997 McVities Penguin Polar Relay was born. It was to be an all women affair with the teams guided by the American, Matty McNair and Canadian, Denise Martin.

"That was the biggest day of my life!"

Daniel's parents moved into her house to take care of the triplets during her four-week absence.

When each team of four women (Daniels was in the first team) completed their stage they were lifted off the ice and replaced with the next team. The challenge was hailed as the first all women's team to reach the North Pole, although of course, the only women to complete the journey from beginning to end were the two guides, Matty McNair and Denise Martin. All the same, it was an extraordinary feat for 'ordinary' women, some who went on to achieve even greater things in Polar adventure.

"When I arrived in the Arctic I just thought how honoured I was to be here. I still had to learn how to ski, something all the other girls already knew how to do, but I felt at one with the ice. I could pull all day, do the cooking and navigate. I thought this is what I am made to do and I didn't want it to end."

On her return and with the cracks already showing in her marriage, Daniels and her husband separated. The traumatic consequences were balanced by the opportunity to plan her next challenge unhindered: a self-guided all female expedition to the South Pole in time for the new Millennium.

Daniels joined forces with Caroline Hamilton, Zoe Hudson, Pom Oliver and Rosie Stancer, who had all completed the McVities North Pole relay.

They had run out of kerosene and were scraping bottom on rations as well. Two biscuits and a chunk of snow made up the day's meal on February 21. "Shall have to make more holes in my belt," recorded Wild tersely. Spencer-Smith minded less: he had lost his appetite, though obsessive thoughts of food plagued him. His breathing came in irregular shallow gasps, and he could no longer stand. Wild hoisted him to his feet and propped him up for bodily functions. He endured the pain and indignity without complaint. "He doesn't howl much like I should," wrote Wild. Mackintosh was too morose to speak. Wild could see from the red stain seeping through the snow over the latrine hole that, like Spencer-Smith, Mackintosh was bleeding from the bowels.

The Lost Men - The Harrowing Story of Shackleton's Ross Sea Party.
Kelly Tyler-Lewis   Published by Bloomsbury

Within three years the band of merry women were ready to roll, with the blessing of their patron, Prince Charles. Flying from Punta Arenas in Chile to Patriot Hills they were finally deposited at Hercules Inlet for the start of their 1,126 km journey, dragging pulks equal to their own body weight, and more.

Sixty days later, with only one resupply along the way, the women skied into the South Pole base to a rapturous welcome by the American base staff. It had been a demanding journey, not only due to the head winds and blizzards they faced but by the end, two of the women were not talking to each other. It is a subject mostly glossed over by the women and the ever-pragmatic Daniels doesn't say more than Rosie Stancer bore the brunt of it.

> *"She had a hard time of it. One member of the team thought she was forgetting things. It manifested itself in the way that one member of the team was having their own difficulties and so they were focusing on someone else's problems. In a team you have to accept that you are all different and everyone has strengths and weaknesses."*

What is important is that the women have not let the clashes overshadow their achievements. In true stoic British tradition the women planted the Union Jack into the snow and sang the National Anthem and Zoe Hudson pulled out a metal stake in the ground that was obstructing the photo session only to discover she had removed the South Pole itself!

Daniels by now was truly bitten by the Polar bug and she was upping the ante. Joining forces with two members of her South Pole team, Caroline Hamilton and Pom Oliver, she set off from Ward Hunt Island on the Canadian coast in March 2002 in an attempt to ski to the North Pole.

Five days into the expedition the women were caught in a ferocious storm that lifted one of the 90 kilos (200 lb) sledges into the air as if it was a piece of flotsam. Unable to put their tent up the women pinned it down with their sledges and crawled underneath the loose fabric whilst tucked into their sleeping bags. The temperature held at -46° C as the storm raged with deafening fury, nearly burying them alive. Other than Daniels digging herself out to send a message on the Argos beacon to the base team, the women remained shivering under their make-do shelter for two long days until the storm had abated.

Surviving their first encounter of the Arctic at its most vicious they heaved and hauled their sledges over towering pressure ridges. At times it would take all three of them to lift and steady just one sledge over the massive blocks of ice. Constant retracing of steps to fetch the other sledges could mean covering three kilometres to gain one.

Oliver's badly frost-bitten feet began to smell with the onset of gangrene. It was looking unlikely that she could continue. On the 47th day the resupply delivered new sledges, clean sleeping bags and food and took back with them a thwarted Oliver. Daniels and Hamilton, distressed at the loss of their companion, never-the-less continued, although Hamilton too was suffering from frostbite.

> *"Caroline had frostbitten fingers, black and blistered and couldn't do anything. Pom (Oliver) had frostbitten hands and feet. I had to dress Caroline and clip her to her sledge. I didn't mind helping clean her bum but I said 'Caroline, have you*

put a hand grenade in here, it looks a bombsite! I will clean you up as much as I can but next time call me at the beginning!'"

The women had two more resupplies by Twin Otter and although the surfaces were flatter their new enemies were the rising temperature, open water and disintegrating ice.

On the 65th day Daniels plunged through the ice into the water. After hauling herself out she took the right course of action by changing her socks, putting plastic bags between her wet boots and dry socks and continuing to ski and haul her sledge to improve plummeting body temperature. But not all of the 81 days spent on the frozen ocean were a catalogue of horrors and Daniel's awe of the Polar region never waned.

On the 1st June Daniels and Hamilton arrived at the top of the world. It was the latest arrival date at the Pole on modern record. Rosie Stancer remained on the ice for longer, 84 days, during her 2007 solo bid but she was air lifted to safety on the 28th May.

Daniels was now ready to try the ultimate challenge. No woman had yet succeeded in skiing to the North Pole on her own. There was one major drawback: she could not raise the £250,000 that would see her nicely off from the Canadian coast with the necessary backing and resupplies she was going to need. So she set about re-mortgaging her house and borrowing the money. There was the cheaper but more difficult option of leaving from Cape Arctichesky on the Siberian side. By sharing flights and resupplies with other teams leaving that year she would manage to bring her expenses down to £50,000.

"I wanted to go from Canada and I wanted to go supported but I couldn't afford a resupply. I knocked on every door and didn't get the money. While it's hell going from Russia, all that mish-mash water, you might be lucky and hit that running and

when you get over that you may have flatter ice. Dominick (Arduin) had died the year before, I hear she went over 30 km of open water and ice."

Finally, in March 2005, Daniels was ready to go. The Arctic window for expeditions does not stay open for long and everything conspired against her. She found herself holed up in Khatanga on the Taymyr Peninsula in Siberia for 15 days while her French air logistics company Cerpolex wrangled with Russian officials over permits, which finally came through.

As is often the case, the ice was deemed too difficult to cross from Arctichesky and she was flown over the unstable ice and dropped at 81∞ 20'. Between her and the North Pole lay 520 nautical miles of moving ice, no more than a shattered glaze over the Arctic Ocean, but with the red tape problems appearing to have been finally resolved, she was thrilled to be on the move. Even the appearance of polar bears couldn't dampen her excitement.

"I hadn't come across bears before. I knew I was going to have an encounter and I saw a mother with two babies. I kept looking at them and I was on tricky ice but I got the video out and got some footage and they moved off. On day four I had a bear stalking around the tent and I felt very vulnerable because I couldn't get my boots on and my feet were cold. I got the gun and shot the ice, then I shot over his head and he ambled off slowly."

The first two weeks were wretchedly cold at -37°C. The euphoria of the departure began to fade as the cold began to bite. Her blistered fingers made even the smallest task painful and unable to warm the tent at night she shook with cold. Yet she never for a moment believed that she could not do it.

What she hadn't bargained on was Cerpolex, the French company in charge of her logistics, falling out with the Russian authorities over the legitimacy of her being there in the first place. The Russian company, Center Polus, operating air logistics in the Arctic, allegedly pulled the rug from under the feet of Cerpolex and demanded that all the expeditions be cancelled. Twenty-one days into the expedition, Daniels' courageous bid for the North Pole was well and truly scuppered.

"I was gutted, sobbing into my sleeping bag. I was desperate. I had gone through two years to do this. It was all about permits and argy-bargy between the two companies."

The attacks and counter attacks continued between Center Polus and Cerpolex long after Daniels and the other teams were picked up off the ice. Today the reasons are no more clearer, other than Cerpolex was accused of ignoring the necessary paper work demanded by the Russians to operate in the area and that they put their clients' safety at risk. The Russian outfit say they offered to take over the running of the expeditions once they were in jeopardy. Daniels says she was never informed of this.

What is clear is that years of training, thousands of pounds and all the aspirations one woman could muster were swallowed up in an instant in a bureaucratic morass.

"But then I thought I have a lot to go back to and I had a fantastic 21 days on the ice. I am not going to spoil it with 'woe is me!"

It is generally agreed that Daniels has what it takes to be the first woman to reach the North Pole solo. The diminutive Rosie Stancer failed in 2007 following an heroic attempt of 84 days on the ice, as did the Amazonian Briton, Hannah McKeand who attempted the same record in 2008. Within two weeks of leaving Ward Hunt Island she was forced to abandon the ice due to shoulder and back injuries sustained when a pressure ridge she was standing on gave way. McKeand, who is over 1.8 metres (6 feet) tall, holds the fastest solo and unsupported ski record of 39 days, 10 hours and 33 minutes from Hercules Inlet to the South Pole.

Unless Daniels finds a sponsor her dream to be the first woman to reach the North Pole solo will remain just that. Presently she is working with Pen Hadow on 'Arctic Survey', a project that plans to measure the thickness of the Polar ice cap.

Her triplets are now 14 years old and she has a five-year-old daughter with her partner, Jo. In the meantime she remains buoyant and, more importantly, fit just in case the opportunity arises for her to get back on the ice alone.

"What I don't want to be doing is crashing around on the ice in my fifties"

Web site: www.anndaniels.com

JOHN WILTON-DAVIES
The Novice Adventurer

"The idea was that if I picked the biggest most challenging thing I could think of then anything else I might think of doing later would seem small and insignificant."

On the 26th November 2006, John Wilton-Davies, 44, a financial advisor and father of two young boys, left Patriot Hills for a solo unsupported walk to the South Pole. Not only was it to be his first experience of setting foot on Antarctica but his first expedition of any kind.

Following his daily dispatches from Antarctica posted on ExplorersWeb, he gave the impression of being down to earth and funny. His list of 'what I should have brought but didn't' mentions an 'extended range snow mobile with CD player, heated hand grips, sheepskin seat and mini bar.'

He was making the trip look somewhat effortless. Here was a man attempting what is considered one of the most difficult challenges on the planet, and if he were to succeed he would be only the ninth person in the world to do so at that time. But there wasn't a peep of angst filtering through his daily dispatches.

Six expeditions set out for the Pole that season, including a Royal Air Force team consisting of four beefy men with the expedition name of Southern Reach, and things weren't going quite so well for them. By the time they were taken off the ice, 162 km short of the Pole, they had lost over 6 kilos each and the expedition leader, WO Alan Sylvester, was flown back to Britain and hospital to have surgery on his frost bitten thumbs.

Although the Royal Air Force team's unsuccessful attempt should not be derided, to state as they did that they aborted their attempt on the Pole 'just like Shackleton' is misleading. Present day Polar adventure with all its modern trappings, cannot compare to the immense hardships (nor the routes) faced by the Edwardian explorers.

When Wilton-Davies finally flew back to England, he bounced through the arrivals hall sun tanned and not an ounce lighter, 'looking like I had just got back from the Bahamas!'

I had two telephone interviews with Wilton-Davies during which he came across as frank and open but what was most puzzling was his insistence that his attempt on the Pole, except for one life threatening incident, was not particularly interesting or challenging.

It was difficult to decide if he was super-human or just plain understated and I needed to put a face to the voice. He lives in a substantial, country house tucked down a narrow lane in Devon. As it turned out he is tall, dark and handsome, with a winning smile and direct manner. He led me through a large playroom scattered with toys and introduced me to his wife, Michele, and his two small boys. She is tall and blonde and they make a striking couple. He is a 'hands on father' and looks after the children on the days his wife works in the City of London, but he is finding everyday domesticity too distracting and is planning to move his home office elsewhere,

As we chatted I think I was beginning to understand what made Wilton-Davies cope with the rigours of his Polar journey. He had the ability to shut down his emotions, a strategy that enabled him to switch onto auto-pilot mode, with only one goal in mind: to get through the day.

The only time he slipped out of his tightly controlled unemotional mindset was when he found himself in a crevasse field, but within days he regained his composure. He conceded there was one enormous drawback to this strategy, by cutting off all emotion he lost the power to tap into the marvels of the expedition. There was no sense of enjoyment or wonder. I suggested, half jokingly, that it might be a survival aid he had learnt as a young child at boarding school, which he half-heartedly laughed at.

He picked the South Pole because he had only the one opportunity of adventure before being reeled back into family life and he decided to go for the optimum experience.

Unable to secure sponsorship he cashed in the £90,000 he had received from selling a property. It would cover all his expenses in reaching the Pole as well as pre-expedition training in Greenland.

> "It was part of my mid-life crisis; I thought if I am going to do anything major in a physical way then this is the time to do it. My wife was quite happy with that as long as it didn't lead me into doing more and more things in the future. I had a window to do one big thing but nothing else later on."

He skied and man hauled his sledge over a distance of 1000 km but with the Pole in his sights, a mere 70 nautical miles away, he was forced to give up. Not because he ran out of steam or food or that he had frost bite but because he ran out of time. The last flight of the season was leaving the Antarctic continent and he had to catch it. If he had had another five days in hand, he would have made it.

The only other unsupported solo attempt that year was by the Briton, Hannah Mckeand. She reached the Pole in a record 39 days , 9 hours and 33 minutes.

Another team called Polar Quest, made up of Royal Navy and Royal Marine personnel (the military were out in force that season), successfully skied and kited to the Pole and back in 71 days Their daily dispatches claimed a tough ride, with one marine reporting, 'the last week has been physically the hardest of my life. At times it has felt impossible that we would ever get to the end of the day let alone the Pole.'

The men, the first British service team to reach the Pole since Scott in 1912, held a memorial service at the Pole to honour Captain Robert Scott and the men who died alongside him. The fact that Scott was a member of the Royal Navy is where the similarity between Polar Quest and Scott end. The words 'emulate' and 'retrace' are frequently bandied about but the all-important fact, that the earlier explorers took much longer and more arduous routes, is overlooked.

Attempts on the Pole during the Edwardian Heroic Age of Shackleton and Scott started from the opposite side of the Antarctic continent, the Ross Sea. Men left on expeditions knowing they would not set foot on home soil again for at least two years. Appalling sea journeys were followed by wintering on the Antarctic coast to await spring and only then could they set out for the Pole. The towering Great Ice Barrier (the Ross Ice Shelf) which extends for hundred of kilometres, and is roughly the size of France, would have to be crossed, followed by man-hauling sledges up the 160 kilometre-long Beardmore Glacier, riveted with crevasses. Above the glacier lies the polar plateau, 3,000 metres above sea level, and still the Pole stands 640 kilometres away.

Wilton-Davies made no claim for anything other than what his expedition was and considering his lack of experience he was close to achieving something extraordinary.

So what made the difference? Hannah McKeand outshone the rest because of experience. She was already an accomplished adventurer, having crossed deserts, climbed mountains and sailed the Southern oceans. She was part of a team that walked to the South Pole two years prior to her solo attempt and she knew what she had to do to clinch the record.

Initially, sorry not to reach the South Pole, Wilton-Davies believed the expedition was more about the 'doing' than the 'reaching'. It was a refreshing viewpoint and one that is seldom voiced.

As time has passed he has changed his views and he admits to feeling a sense of disappointment that the Pole was tantalizingly close.

> "Now that I am back and my brain has remembered ordinary life at home, it was a wasted opportunity not to push a little bit harder. At the end of the day, the hardest part was the boredom and if you are bored it is hard to motivate yourself."

If he had taken a guide his success would have been as good as guaranteed. He lost three days while waiting in Chile for better weather conditions to land in Antarctica and another three days when he found himself in an area of crevasses, forcing him to turn around and go north again. To top it all he was tent bound for two and half days with bad weather. It would have been a guide's job to calculate these variables and motivate his client to make up the time.

> "The main interest I had in the whole expedition was the experience of what I was going to be doing and whether I got to the Pole was important but of secondary importance. To spend 60 days with someone I didn't know wasn't that appealing; people say its harder doing it on your own but I didn't take that view. I didn't want the risk of falling out with someone I didn't really know and having to spend the next two months with them."

On a personal level he believes he achieved more walking a thousand kilometres on his own than walking eleven hundred kilometres with a professional guide. He is adamant the journey was easier than he anticipated, much of it endlessly tedious as he trudged day in and day out towards his goal. He never felt the cold but simply ran out of things to think about.

> "Anyone who does something like that has to sound enthusiastic about their

experience because they have had sponsors etc. I think people exaggerate the weather because it's what people expect to hear. I was never cold on the entire expedition and it was rare I could sleep in my sleeping bag it; was too hot."

Yet members on other expeditions that year, as in the team Southern Reach, did suffer from frostbite. Team Polar Quest lost in total more than 56 kilos body weight.

When I challenged Wilton-Davies that he might have confused boredom with loneliness he disagreed. However, some months later when we spoke again, he remembered things differently. He now accepts that during the latter weeks of the expedition the Pole seemed less important because he was tired and lonely.

"I didn't expect to have a problem. I didn't mind being on my own except when I started to get into trouble. I had a dodgy period when I got stuck in a crevasse area, which was very scary, and being with someone else would have been a great help."

The day before Christmas he wandered into an area of disturbed ice and found himself walking on a ridge, which swept away into valleys on either side. The floors of the valleys were puckered with holes and crevasses. He came down off the ridge to investigate and decided it would be folly to continue along the valley floor and his safest option would be

to climb back up on to the ridge. His sledge was too heavy to heave up the incline and he was forced to unload half of its contents before setting off. Once on top of the ridge he set his tent up then descended to the valley floor to collect the rest of his belongings. Wilton-Davies held his nerve but back in his tent there was no easy sleep.

Christmas Day dawned with the full horror of his predicament. He found it impossible to move along the side of the hills without his sledge capsizing. There was nothing for it but to descend to the valley floor, which was in fact a glacier. To help manoeuvre his sledge he clipped it only two feet behind him instead of the usual 10 or 12 feet and then he broke the second rule, he took off his skis.

Without warning one of his legs dropped through a fissure in the snow, below him he could see a gaping blue hole and he knew he was on top of a crevasse and balancing on a snow bridge that could break at any moment, plunging him into the abyss below. True to the British manner of understatement, he coolly described finding himself in a situation that would chill even the most seasoned Polar explorer.

> *"I had done my homework pretty thoroughly. Generally speaking you get a type of crevasse in Antarctica which is very big and very obvious and generally pretty safe to walk across because they have been filled with snow the last five hundred years and one little guy with his sledge walking across them isn't going to make much difference. I came across crevasses like that several times.*
> *Where I did have a problem was when crevasses had no surface evidence at all, they were much smaller, three to twenty feet across and had no edges to them. You didn't know you were on them until you had a problem.*
> *I couldn't afford to leave behind my sledge and pulling it up more than five degrees becomes difficult and the only way I could get control in that terrain was to take my skis off but as soon as you take your skis off, the pressure you apply on the ground per square inch, becomes that much greater because you are not spreading your weight."*

No sooner had he gathered himself up than his leg went through a snow bridge for the second time. Thinking his sledge could drop into the crevasse and take him with it, he unclipped it and jumped aside. He was now in a serious predicament. Everything he needed to survive was in the sledge, but by going back to retrieve it he might fall into the crevasse. With a pounding heart he gingerly picked his way back to the sledge and pulled it to a safer place, set up camp and telephoned ALE at the Patriot Hills base on his satellite phone.

They advised him to retrace his steps the following day. Wilton-Davies admits to having to muster all his courage the following morning to set out again. His foot broke through into crevasses on two more occasions. Providence was with him.

> *"On four occasions, one leg went through the snow bridge into the crevasse and by pure luck nothing else did. If I had fallen into one I wouldn't be talking to you today. When your leg goes through and you are several hundred miles away from the nearest person, it's quite scary!*

Being a novice in Antarctica, I wasn't really sure whether this strange bit of terrain with these hills, valleys and crevasses was a normal feature or if I was unlucky to stumble across it and should try and find a way round it. I just found more of the same where ever I went so I took the decision to plough on ahead and it was only after those experiences I thought that this isn't right, it's too dangerous."

Often enough the dogs broke through the snow-bridges on the morning of the 23rd, but only once were matters serious, when Ninnis's sledge, doubtless on account of its extra weight, again broke through a lid of snow and was securely jammed in a crevasse just below the surface. On this occasion we were in a serious predicament, for the sledge was in such a position that an unskillful movement would have sent it hurling into the chasm below. So the unpacking of the load was a tedious and delicate operation. The freight consisted chiefly of large, soldered tins, packed tightly with dried seal meat. Each of these weighed about ninety pounds and all were most securely roped to the sledge. The sledge was got up and reloaded without the loss of a single tin, and once more we breathed freely. A valley almost free of crevasses was chosen as the upward track to the plateau. We threw in our weight hauling with the dogs, and had a long, steep drag over furrowed neve, pitching the tent after a day's journey of twelve miles.

Douglas Mawson *The Home of the Blizzard*

Success of Polar expeditions is founded on layer upon layer of gained experience. Today's most successful Polar adventurers can only raise the game because they have a wealth of past experience on which they base calculated risks.

   Wilton-Davies had very little experience to draw on. He didn't recognise the potentially dangerous terrain he found himself in until it was too late. Luck rather than good judgement saved him.

"I was certainly haunted by them for some days afterwards but now I don't think I over or under-reacted. I appreciate I was unlucky to be there in the first place but lucky to have survived breaking through as many time as I did."

He has been both lauded and criticised for his walk to the South Pole: applauded for his daring and pluck and censured for attempting a journey which could have led to his death. He has been criticised for being irresponsible and encouraging would-be adventurers to attempt expeditions without the necessary experience.

   Of course it can also be said that Wilton-Davies took responsibility for his own actions and that his courage, tenacity, and 'no frills' attitude, all the qualities that are so often lacking in our over cosseted life styles, is an inspiration to all.

"I think someone with the level of experience I had and going out trying to do what I did, is quite dangerous and to be honest that is what appealed to me.

I wanted to do something that was very difficult, to test myself to the limits. Whether that would encourage people to take risks is another matter. I was given a very distinct impression by the experts that there are sufficient safeguards in place, mainly through ALE. In other words ALE safeguards would stop people going but to what extent commercial interests might take over I have no idea. One of the experiences I took out of the whole affair was that the environment down there, for me, was no way near as bad as I was led to believe. If that leads to people doing things they are not prepared for then of course that is very bad news. The only way you can get there realistically is with ALE and they won't let you do it if you are an idiot.

I don't want to see people hurting themselves but when I was out there people on last degree and two degree trips were all coming back with frostbite. Some people do go down there with such a strong desire to achieve the Pole that they push on. I went out thinking this was going to be a fantastic experience; lets see what happens.

Almost certainly it would not have happened had I had a guide. I had insufficient knowledge to judge if it was the sort of terrain I should have been walking in. If you are asking me, with hindsight, which is better, to have taken a guide and made it or to do what I did, I think I personally achieved more."

It was a momentous decision to try and reach the South Pole solo and unsupported and Wilton-Davies nearly pulled it off. Does he believe the £90,000 was well spent? Absolutely. Did it have the desired effect of satisfying his hunger for adventure? No, if anything it had whetted his appetite.

"I went out expecting not to enjoy it and I didn't enjoy it. The pleasure comes afterwards from having done the experience. It's a very boring exercise walking to the Pole, the terrain is largely the same almost all the way. The enjoyment of the trip will become more apparent as time goes by. It was worth spending the money and it was a great adventure and I am glad I did it."

I telephoned Wilton-Davies several months later to enquire how he was settling down to which he answered not very well and that he was gathering his courage to tell Michele, his wife, that he was planning another expedition. A few weeks later an email arrived.

"Well, amazingly, Michele is totally behind my plans - perhaps I should be worried?
The plan is to attempt a solo unsupported walk from Hercules Inlet to the South Pole (yes, I know that's what I nearly did last time) but then to turn around and come back again - still unsupported. I am calling it the Last Great Challenge."

Web site: www.lastgreatchallenge.com

GLOSSARY

ARGOS BEACON - an emergency transmission and tracking device that sends out signals and can work at -40° C. Used to follow the migration of whales it is popular with polar adventurers.

CREVASSE - a fracture in a glacier

DRIFT ICE - sea ice that floats on the surface of the water, carried along by winds and sea currents.

FAST ICE - frozen sea ice along the coasts extending out to sea. Unlike drift ice it does not move with the currents and winds.

FROST NIP - superficial freezing of the skin.

GPS - global satellite navigation system, the size of a mobile telephone, which calculates position, i.e. latitude and longitude or location on a map.

ICE RUBBLE - ice blocks thrown up by colliding ice flows.

KABATIC WINDS - fierce winds that blow down a slope, particularly over ice sheets found in Antarctica and Greenland.

LEAD - open water caused by cracks in the pack ice on the Arctic Ocean.

MORAINE - debris of soil and rock found in glaciers.

NEGATIVE DRIFT - drift in the opposite direction of travel; caused by ocean currents.

PARASAIL/KITE & SKI-KITING - kites varying in size depending on wind strength which are attached to a harness worn by the skier and controlled by lines and a bar or handle. A popular method used to cross great distances.

PRESSURE RIDGE - ridges formed from broken compressed pieces of first year ice. Thickness can vary greatly.

PULK - a light carbon fibre sledge used for pulling supplies

RESUPPLIES/SUPPORTED - extra food and equipment brought in during an expedition.

SASTRUGI - small hillocks of snow formed by the wind.

SLEDGE/SLED - often used instead of the name pulk; a sledge is usually pulled by dogs.

SOLO - Single-handed

SNOW BRIDGE - an arc of compact snow that covers a crevasse, sometimes weight-bearing but can break with any pressure on it.

UNSUPPORTED - no physical assistance from outside, such as food drops, replaced equipment, an evacuation, an airlift or motorized transport.

The North and South Poles lie at 90 degrees. There are 60 minutes in a degree of latitude, based on one nautical mile. A nautical mile equals one minute, therefore the distance from eighty degrees to the Pole is 600 miles.

LIST OF PHOTOGRAPHERS

If you enjoyed reading Ice Tracks,
here are details of more books about great Antarctic ordeals and treks.
These and other Antarctic titles are available from:

The Erskine Press, The White House, Eccles, Norwich NR16 2PB
01953 887277
erskpes@aol.com   WWW.ERSKINE-PRESS.COM

EIGHT MEN IN A CRATE
Anthea Arnold

In February 1956 eight young men stood on the Filchner Ice Shelf and waved goodbye to the *Theron* as it sailed away. They were the advance party of the Trans-Antarctic Expedition of 1955-1957, headed by Vivian Fuchs and Sir Edmund Hillary.

Their job was to build accommodation, explore and lay depots to ease the passage of Fuch's team the following year.

The eight men only just survived an awful Antarctic winter, living by day in a sno-cat crate and sleeping in tents at night while trying to erect a poorly designed hut with inadequate manpower and equipment. The loss of much of their stores put their survival on a knife edge. This account, based on the diary of Rainer Goldsmith, the young medical officer, shows how close to disaster they came and how lucky they were to survive. Fuchs later admitted that:

> …apart from Scott's marooned Northern Party theirs was the most severe ordeal in the history of Antarctic exploration.

160pp with 25 b&w maps and illustrations and 16pp colour photographs   **£12.75**

THE WICKED MATE
The Antarctic Diary of Victor Campbell
Edited by H.G.R. King

In 1910 Captain Robert Falcon Scott sent six men, the Northern Party, under the command of Lieutenant Victor Campbell, to explore along the coast of King Edward VII Land. After a successful ten months at Cape Adare they moved to Inexpressible Island, as stormy and desolate a place as could be found anywhere in the world. The failure of the relief ship to collect them at the end of the summer left them marooned with no hut and little food. Campbell kept all the men alive in a snow cave 12' x 9'. He drew an imaginary line down the middle of the cave. One side represented the officer's wardroom, the other the men's mess deck and such was the discipline that the enlisted men could say what they wanted on their side of the line, as could the officers on theirs. Each group turned a deaf ear to the other.

After the winter, in October 1912, Campbell led them over 230 miles of sea ice back to the base at Cape Evans, only to learn of the fate of Captain Scott and the Pole party.

Its focus is a saga of endurance that should be counted
among the most famous exploits in Polar history

192pp, hardback, jacketed, over 75 photographs and illustrations **£24.95**

ELEPHANT ISLAND & BEYOND
The Life and Diaries of Thomas Orde Lees

The story of Ernest Shackleton's 1914 *Endurance* expedition and its aftermath is well known. What is not so well known is the part played by Thomas Orde Lees in keeping Shackleton's crew alive during their ordeal.

Not only was Orde Lees disliked simply for being himself, but he was also expected to become the first victim for cannibalism if the 22 men on Elephant Island had run out of food. Lees's diary is a harrowing tale of survival and perhaps now his part in keeping the men alive during their ordeal can now be recognised.

The book includes many previously unpublished photographs as well as a detailed account of his quite extraordinary life after Antarctica.

320pp, 254 x 195mm, hardback, jacketed, 0ver 40 photographs and drawings **£24.95**

IN THE TEETH OF THE WIND
South Through the Pole

Alain Hubert & Dixie Dansercoer with Michael Brent

In November 1997 two Belgian explorers crossed the Antarctic continent from the Weddell Sea to the Ross Sea on foot. From Dronning Maud Land Alain Hubert and Dixie Dansercoer travelled for 99 days until they reached the American base at McMurdo Sound, some 3920 kilometres away. By using traction sales, specially designed for the expedition, they set many records, managing on some days to clock up distances of over 100 kilometres at amazing speeds.
This full colour book contains over 90 pictures of their trip, as well as many maps and drawings.

...an extraordinary journey across this most inhospitable of continents...
full of danger and excitement. The pictures illustrate the trials of the journey and the
awesome beauty of...Antarctica.

224 pp, hardback, jacketed, full colour throughout £24.95 reduced to **£10.00**

Please add £2.50 to each order for post